MANAGERIAL ACCOUNTING PROJECTS

Using Microsoft® Office

competency based

ROGER A. GEE
San Diego Mesa College

South-Western College Publishing
Thomson Learning

Australia • Canada • Mexico • Singapore • Spain • United Kingdom • United States

Managerial Accounting Projects Using Microsoft® Office by Roger A. Gee
Acquisitions Editor: Sharon Oblinger
Marketing Manager: Larry Qualls
Production Editor: Heather Mann
Manufacturing Coordinator: Doug Wilke
Cover Design: Rick Moore

Printed in the United States of America
1 2 3 4 5 03 02 01 00

For more information contact South-Western College Publishing, 5101 Madison Road, Cincinnati, Ohio, 45227 or find us on the Internet at http://www.swcollege.com

For permission to use material from this text or product, contact us by
• **telephone: 1-800-730-2214**
• **fax: 1-800-730-2215**
• **web: http://www.thomsonrights.com**

ISBN: 0-324-02824-5

This book is printed on acid-free paper.

Message to Students

This workbook is designed to help you apply the accounting concepts discussed in your Managerial Accounting textbook. Workbook projects cover the following themes:

- Product costing and decision making
- Control measurements and evaluation
- Internal control and reciprocal costs

While you are completing the projects, you will also learn a competency which the Labor Secretary's Commission on Achieving the Necessary Skills [SCANS] found to be essential for success in the labor force. You will learn how to think while integrating spreadsheet, word processing, and presentation software. These computer skills are required in all good accounting, finance, marketing, and management jobs.

Each project has a section of required steps. Make sure that you complete the steps in order. Key verbs in the steps are underlined. Procedures in the Appendix are alphabetized by underlined verbs.

Project 13 requires you to participate in a group of three or more students. You will solve a problem that has no clear correct answer. You may be required to report the results of your work to the class using presentation software. You will also submit a report on three local businesses using word processing software.

Some of the projects are more complex than the material shown in your textbook. One reason is that you sometimes have to illustrate reports and presentations differently when integrating software packages. Another reason is that this workbook is meant to add value to what you learn from your textbook.

Take your time, and enjoy your projects!

Roger A. Gee
San Diego Mesa College

Thanks to the students in my Summer and Fall 1999 managerial accounting classes. They tested all of the projects in this workbook. I appreciate each error they found and every suggestion for improvement.

Contents

- Integrate *Microsoft® Excel* and *Microsoft® Word* to create a report that describes variance analysis of variable manufacturing costs.
- Apply what-if analysis of three scenarios using a variance analysis worksheet.

- Integrate *Microsoft® Excel* and *Microsoft® Word* to create a report that describes measures used to evaluate the performance of two production departments.
- Apply what-if analysis at different levels of sales revenue using a performance evaluation worksheet.

- Integrate *Microsoft® Excel* and *Microsoft® PowerPoint* to create a presentation that proposes the implementation of a just-in-time manufacturing system.
- Explain how a just-in-time manufacturing system can improve the return on assets when it is installed.

- Integrate *Microsoft® Excel* and *Microsoft® Word* to create a report that explains and demonstrates capital investment decisions using the following methods: net present value, internal rate of return, payback period, and accounting rate of return.
- Apply what-if analysis at different levels of sales revenue using a capital-investment-proposal worksheet.

- Integrate *Microsoft® Excel* and *Microsoft® Word* to create a report that discusses internal control areas of concern if a company switches to a management information system that features paperless accounting software.
- Appraise the control system in a paperless accounting system using a segmented income statement.

- Integrate *Microsoft® Excel* and *Microsoft® PowerPoint* to create a presentation that explains and demonstrates the step-down and simultaneous algebraic equation methods for allocating reciprocal support costs.
- Modify a cost allocation worksheet to include a new revenue-producing department and evaluate the differences in cost allocation using two methods of calculation.

Project One

Financial Versus Managerial Accounting

Competencies

- Use *Microsoft®* *PowerPoint* to create a presentation that compares and contrasts financial accounting and managerial accounting.
- Describe how managerial accounting affects the job you have or plan to have using at least two examples.

Project Data

Slide 1. Title and sub-titles are illustrated.

Title 44 pt. Sub-title 32 pt.	**Financial Accounting Versus Managerial Accounting** By Student's Name

Slide 2.   Title: Topics for Discussion
    Bulleted list: Similarities between financial accounting and managerial accounting
                    Differences between financial accounting and managerial accounting

Slide 3.   Title: Similarities Between Financial and Managerial Accounting
    Bulleted list: Both contain the word *accounting*
                    Both use reports as primary communication devices
                    Both use the same rules of debit and credit

Slide 4.   Titles: First Four Differences
                    Financial Accounting vs. Managerial Accounting
        Left text: Reports to outsiders   Right text: Reports to insiders

Slide 5.   Titles: First Four Differences
                    Financial Accounting vs. Managerial Accounting
            Left text: Reports to outsiders   Right text: Reports to insiders
                    Reports summarize   Reports for decisions
                        past activities   affecting the future

Slide 6.   Titles: First Four Differences
                    Financial Accounting vs. Managerial Accounting
            Left text: Reports to outsiders   Right text: Reports to insiders
                    Reports summarize   Reports for decisions
                        past activities   affecting the future
                    Report data must be   Report data must be
                        objective & verifiable   relevant & flexible

Slide 7.   Titles: First Four Differences
                    Financial Accounting vs. Managerial Accounting
            Left text: Reports to outsiders   Right text: Reports to insiders
                    Reports summarize   Reports for decisions
                        past activities   affecting the future
                    Report data must be   Report data must be
                        objective & verifiable   relevant & flexible
                    Precision of report   Timeliness of report
                        information is required   information is required

Slide 8.   Titles: Three More Differences
                    Financial Accounting vs. Managerial Accounting
            Left text: Reports summarize   Right text: Reports detail data
                        data for entire entity   about entity segments

Slide 9.   Titles: Three More Differences
                    Financial Accounting vs. Managerial Accounting
            Left text: Reports summarize   Right text: Reports detail data
                        data for entire entity   about entity segments
                    Reports must follow   Reports don't have to
                        GAAP   follow GAAP

Slide 10.   Titles: Three More Differences
                    Financial Accounting vs. Managerial Accounting
            Left text: Reports summarize   Right text: Reports detail data
                        data for entire entity   about entity segments
                    Reports must follow   Reports don't have to
                        GAAP   follow GAAP
                    Mandatory reports   No mandatory reports

Slide 11.   Title: Conclusion
    Bulleted list: Most important similarity
                     Most important difference

Slide 12.   Title: That's All, Folks!

The speech part of the 12-slide presentation is as follows:

1.   Ladies and Gentlemen: My name is Student's Name. Today, I am going to compare and contrast financial accounting and managerial accounting.

2.   This means that I am going to discuss the similarities and differences. When I discuss similarities between financial and managerial accounting, I will compare them. When I point out differences between financial and managerial accounting, I will contrast the two types of accounting. You will see that there are some similarities, but more differences.

3.   There are three similarities between financial and managerial accounting. The first similarity is the word *accounting*. Accounting can be defined as the art of communicating economic information about a business, government agency, or not-for-profit association. Second, reports are the chief devices for communicating information in both. Third, the same rules of debit and credit are used to record the financial information.

4.   There are many differences. The first difference addresses the intended audience. In financial accounting, the reports are primarily prepared for...[Explain and give example]. In managerial accounting, the reports are primarily prepared for...[Explain and give example].

5.   The second difference has to do with the purpose of the reports. The reports in financial accounting summarize information about...[Explain and give example]. The reports in managerial accounting are for...[Explain and give example].

6.   The third difference has to do with report data. The reports prepared for financial accounting purposes must be...[Explain and give example]. The reports prepared for managerial accounting purposes must be...[Explain and give example].

7.   The fourth difference has to do with the information in the reports. In financial accounting, the reports emphasize...[Explain and give example]. Reports in managerial accounting emphasize...[Explain and give example].

8.   The fifth difference has to do with the level of detail in the reports. Reports in financial accounting summarize data for the entity as a whole. For example, a single number for *cash* on the balance sheet may summarize the balances of 100 different checking accounts. Reports in managerial accounting can detail data about entity segments such as divisions, regions, districts, stores, factories, departments, shifts, and even individuals.

9. The sixth difference has to do with conforming with generally accepted accounting principles. In financial accounting, the reports <u>must</u> be in conformity with GAAP. Each annual report contains an auditor's letter that says so. In managerial accounting, the reports don't have to conform with GAAP. For example, there is no way that a budget containing estimates of future operations can conform with GAAP.

10. The seventh difference has to do with whether or not external reports are mandatory. In financial accounting, external reports are mandatory. The SEC requires periodic reports from corporations that issue "publicly traded" stock. The IRS requires reports from all businesses. In managerial accounting, there are no mandatory reports. Reports are generated on an "as need" basis.

11. In conclusion, I compared and contrasted financial and managerial accounting in this presentation. The most important similarity is…[Give your opinion]. The most important difference is…[Give your opinion].

12. Thanks for your attention. Do you have any questions?

Required

Make sure that you complete the following steps in order. Refer to the procedures in the Appendix, which are alphabetized by underlined verb. Note the underlined verbs in the steps below.

---

1. <u>Open</u> *PowerPoint* and create a *title slide* using the data in the exhibit.
2. <u>Apply</u> a slide color scheme. Use a blue background.
3. <u>Insert</u> a *bulleted list* format for slides 2 – 3.
4. <u>Insert</u> a *2-column text* format for slides 4 – 10. Hint: When you are finished with slide 4, insert a duplicate slide to create slide 5.
5. <u>Insert</u> a *bulleted list* format for slide 11.
6. <u>Insert</u> a *title only* format for slide 12.
7. <u>Apply</u> *dissolve* as a slide transition effect for slides 2 – 4, 8, 11, and 12.
8. <u>Apply</u> *fly from bottom* as text preset animation for slides 3 and 11.
9. <u>Apply</u> *speech text* to slides 1 – 12.
10. Complete your speech based upon information in Chapter M1 of the textbook.
11. <u>Insert</u> footers on the notes pages.
12. <u>Save</u> your project to a floppy disk according to the procedure in Appendix A.
13. <u>Print</u> the presentation as *notes pages.*
14. Staple the Transmittal Sheet on top of the notes pages.
15. Describe on the Transmittal Sheet how managerial accounting affects the job you have or plan to have. Use at least two examples.

Project One Transmittal Sheet

Student Name: _____

Student Identification Number: _____

Class: _____

Date: _____

_____
_____
_____
_____
_____
_____
_____
_____
_____
_____
_____
_____
_____
_____
_____
_____
_____
_____
_____
_____
_____
_____
_____
_____
_____

Notes:

Project Two

Variable and Fixed Costs

Competencies

- Use *Microsoft® Excel* to describe and chart fixed and variable costs and to estimate those costs using the high-low and least-squares regression methods.
- Explain the changes in variable and fixed cost calculations when output and manufacturing costs are changed.

Project Data

Sheet 1. Cost data

	A	B	C	D	E	F	G
1							
2		STUDENT'S NAME CORPORATION					
3		VARIABLE AND					
4.		FIXED COSTS					
5		YEAR ENDED DECEMBER 31, THIS YEAR					
6							
7		DEFINITIONS					
8		Variable costs are costs that change in total with volume (units of production).					
9		They remain fixed on a per-unit basis.					
10		Fixed costs are costs that do not change in total with volume (units of					
11		production). They vary on a per-unit basis.					
12		Widgets are hypothetical products manufactured in a fictitious company.					
13							
14		COST DATA					
15		Number of widgets	0	4,000	8,000	12,000	
16		Cost per unit	$5.00				
17		Fixed costs	$60,000				
18							

Sheet 1. Chart calculations: Use cell-based formulas for all amounts shown.

	A	B	C	D	E	F	G
19		CHART CALCULATIONS					
20			0	4,000	8,000	12,000	
21		Variable costs	$0	$20,000	$40,000	$60,000	
22		Fixed costs	$60,000	$60,000	$60,000	$60,000	
23		Total costs	$60,000	$80,000	$100,000	$120,000	

Sheet 1. Chart: Use XY scatter with data points connected by lines.

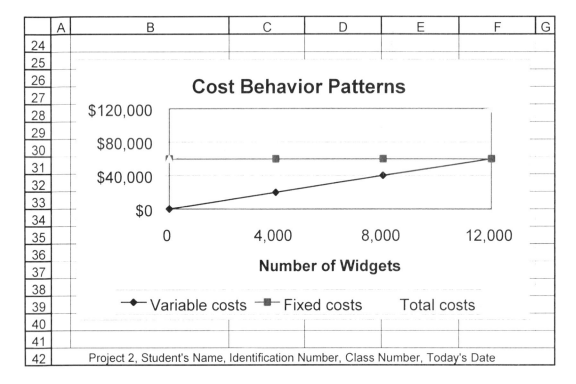

	A	B	C	D	E	F	G
24							
25							
26			Cost Behavior Patterns				
27							
28		$120,000					
29							
30		$80,000					
31							
32		$40,000					
33							
34		$0					
35		0	4,000	8,000	12,000		
36							
37		Number of Widgets					
38							
39		Variable costs Fixed costs Total costs					
40							
41							
42		Project 2, Student's Name, Identification Number, Class Number, Today's Date					

Sheet 2. Cost data

	A	B	C	D	E	F	G
1							
2		STUDENT'S NAME CORPORATION					
3		HIGH-LOW METHOD FOR ESTIMATING					
4		VARIABLE AND FIXED COSTS					
5		YEAR ENDED DECEMBER 31, THIS YEAR					
6							
7		HOW IT WORKS					
8		The high-low method is used to estimate variable and fixed costs based on					
9		contrasting units of production and costs at high and low activity levels.					
10		The variable cost per unit is computed by dividing the difference in costs					
11		by the difference in units of production. On this worksheet, the fixed cost					
12		per unit is computed by subtracting the variable cost at the highest level					
13		from the total cost at the highest level.					
14							
15		COST DATA					
16			1st Qtr	2nd Qtr	3rd Qtr	4th Qtr	
17		Number of widgets	4,000	12,000	8,000	0	
18		Total manufacturing costs	$80,000	$120,000	$100,000	$60,000	
19							

Sheet 2. Cost calculations: Use cell-based formulas for all amounts shown.

	A	B	C	D	E	F	G
20		COST CALCULATIONS	Highest	Lowest	Difference		
21			Activity	Activity	Observed		
22		Number of widgets	12,000	0	12,000		
23		Total manufacturing costs	$120,000	$60,000	$60,000		
24							
25		Variable cost per unit...			$5.00		
26		Fixed cost per unit:					
27		Total manufacturing costs at highest activity level......			$120,000		
28		Less variable cost at highest level............................			60,000		
29							
30		Total fixed cost..			$60,000		

Sheet 2. Chart calculations: Use cell-based formulas for all amounts shown.

	A	B	C	D	E	F	G
32		CHART CALCULATIONS					
33			4,000	12,000	8,000	0	
34		Variable costs	$20,000	$60,000	$40,000	$0	
35		Fixed costs	$60,000	$60,000	$60,000	$60,000	
36		Total costs	$80,000	$120,000	$100,000	$60,000	

Sheet 2. Chart: Use XY scatter with data points connected by lines.

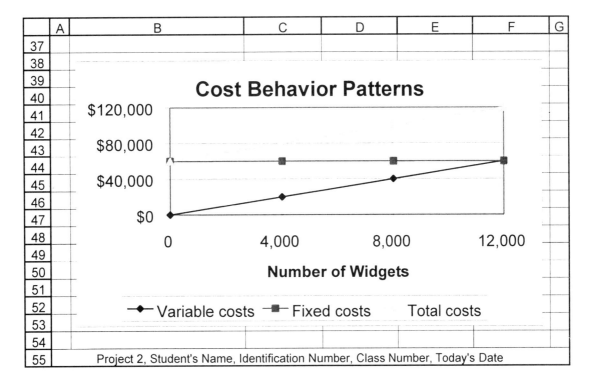

-2.3-

Sheet 3. Cost data

	A	B	C	D	E	F	G
1							
2		STUDENT'S NAME CORPORATION					
3		LEAST-SQUARES REGRESSION METHOD					
4		FOR DETERMINING VARIABLE AND FIXED COSTS					
5		YEAR ENDED DECEMBER 31, THIS YEAR					
6							
7		HOW IT WORKS					
8		The least-squares regression method uses the INTERCEPT function to calculate where the					
9		total cost (regression) line is placed on a chart. The INTERCEPT function minimizes the					
10		sum of the squared errors between the acutal data points representing total manufacturing					
11		costs and the line. The point where the total cost line intercepts the Y axis is equal to the					
12		fixed costs. The scattergraph method is the manual eqivalent of this method. It is not as					
13		accurate because the total cost line has to be drawn through the data points by hand.					
14							
15		COST DATA					
16			1st Qtr	2nd Qtr	3rd Qtr	4th Qtr	
17		Number of widgets	4,000	0	12,000	8,000	
18		Total manufacturing costs (data points)	$80,000	$60,000	$120,000	$100,000	
19							

Sheet 3. Cost calculations: Use cell-based formulas for all amounts shown.

	A	B	C	D	E	F	G
19							
20		COST CALCULATIONS					
21		Total cost of first quarter widgets	$80,000	The function in cell C22			
22		Less fixed cost	60,000	=INTERCEPT(C18:F18,C17:F17)			
23				calculates where the total cost line			
24		Variable cost of first quarter widgets	$20,000	intercepts the Y axis.			
25		Variable cost per widget	$5.00				
26							

Sheet 3. Chart calculations: Use cell-based formulas for all amounts shown.

	A	B	C	D	E	F	G
26							
27		CHART CALCULATIONS					
28			4,000	0	12,000	8,000	
29		Variable cost	$20,000	$0	$60,000	$40,000	
30		Fixed cost	$60,000	$60,000	$60,000	$60,000	
31		Total cost	$80,000	$60,000	$120,000	$100,000	
32							

Sheet 3. Chart: Use XY scatter with data points connected by lines.

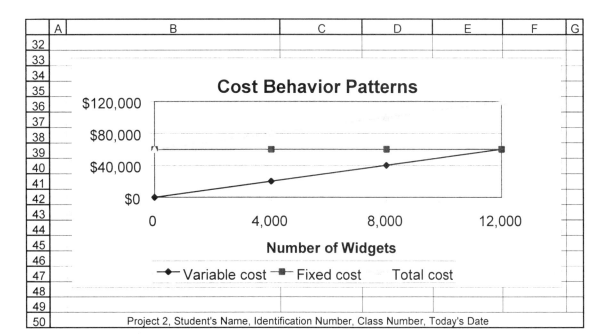

Required

Make sure that you complete the following steps in order. Refer to the procedures in the Appendix, which are alphabetized by underlined verb. Note the underlined verbs in the steps below.

1. <u>Open</u> *Excel* and create three worksheets that look like the examples in the project. <u>Merge</u> and center text in rows 2 – 5 and the last row of each worksheet. Use your name in place of the words *student's name*. Use numbers for the actual year in place of the words *this year*. <u>Enter</u> cell-based formulas and functions to calculate all amounts except those in the cost data sections. <u>Create</u> a chart in each worksheet. <u>Format</u> each worksheet.
2. <u>Save</u> your project to a floppy disk.
3. <u>Print</u> the workbook.
4. Record the Sheet 1 total costs on the Transmittal Sheet. Change the cost per unit in cell C16 to $4.80. Change the fixed costs in cell C17 to $62,000. Record the new total costs on the Transmittal Sheet. Which set of total costs is better for Student's Name Corporation?
5. Record the Sheet 2 variable cost per unit and the total fixed cost on the Transmittal Sheet. Change the number of widgets in cell D17 to 11,500. Record the new variable cost per unit and new total fixed cost on the Transmittal. Which set of costs is better for Student's Name Corporation? Why?

6. Record the Sheet 3 cost calculations on the Transmittal Sheet. Increase the 1st quarter output from 4,000 widgets to 6,500 widgets. Also, increase the 1st quarter manufacturing costs from $80,000 to $91,200. Record the new cost calculations on the Transmittal Sheet. Which set of costs is better for Student's Name Corporation?
7. Copy each worksheet.
8. Print each worksheet copy to show the formulas.
9. Staple the Transmittal Sheet on top of the three original worksheets and the three worksheet copies that show the formulas.

Project Two Transmittal Sheet

Student Name: _____

Student Identification Number: _____

Class: _____

Date: _____

_____
_____
_____
_____
_____
_____
_____
_____
_____
_____
_____
_____
_____
_____
_____
_____
_____
_____
_____
_____
_____
_____

Notes:

Project Three

Job-Order Costing Versus Process Costing

Competencies

- Use *Microsoft® Word* to create a two-page report that compares and contrasts job-order costing versus process costing.
- List five products that are probably made using a job-order costing system and five products that are probably made using a process costing system.

Job-Order Costing Data

A. Used when different products, jobs, or batches are produced each accounting period
B. A job-order number is used on all documents that help accumulate product costs
   1. Materials requisition form—used to order direct materials
   2. Time tickets—used to record direct labor hours
   3. Job cost sheet—used to calculate direct materials, direct labor, and manufacturing overhead costs for each job

Process Costing Data

A. Used when homogeneous products are produced over a long period of time
B. Costs are accumulated by department rather than job-order number
C. A production report is used instead of a job cost sheet

General Costing Data

A. Three types of manufacturing costs are used in job-order and process costing
   1. Direct materials: go into final product, can be raw materials or components
   2. Direct labor: employee costs that can be traced to product, assembly-line labor
   3. Manufacturing overhead: factory costs such as indirect labor, depreciation, maintenance and repair, insurance, property taxes, utilities
B. Nonmanufacturing costs are kept separate in job-order and process costing
   1. Marketing or selling costs
   2. General and administrative costs
C. The same account names are used in job-order and process costing
   1. Direct (or Raw) materials inventory
   2. Work-in-process inventory
   3. Finished goods inventory
   4. Manufacturing (or Factory) overhead

D. Just-in-time (JIT) costing can be used in job-order and process costing
E. Activity-based costing (ABC), used to calculate manufacturing overhead, is more important in job-order costing than in process costing

Required

> **Make sure that you complete the following steps in order. Refer to the procedures in the Appendix, which are alphabetized by underlined verb. Note the underlined verbs in the steps below.**

1. Open *Word* and create a two-page report that compares and contrasts job-order costing versus process costing. The title of the report is *Job-Order Costing Versus Process Costing by Student's Name*. This report should have three elements: introduction, main body, and conclusion. In the introduction, tell the reader that Student's Name Corporation owns two manufacturing plants. One plant manufactures custom products [name the hypothetical products] and uses a job-order cost system. The other plant manufactures generic products [name the products] and uses a process cost system. The introduction should be short— three or four sentences. The main body is used to present your facts in a logical manner. It is here that you compare (show similarities) and contrast (show differences) between job-order costing and process costing. Use examples from Student's Name Corporation (your hypothetical company). The conclusion should be short—three or four sentences. You are allowed your opinion here. For example, you can indicate the most important similarity and the most important difference between job-order costing and process costing in your company. Refer to Chapter 3 in the textbook for information.
2. Insert footers into the *Word* document.
3. Save your project to a floppy disk.
4. Print the *Word* document (your report).
5. Staple the Transmittal Sheet on top of the document.
6. On the Transmittal Sheet, list five products that are probably made using a job-order costing system and five products that are probably made using a process costing system. Some examples are listed in Chapter M3 of the Ingram textbook.

Project Three Transmittal Sheet

Student Name: _____

Student Identification Number: _____

Class: _____

Date: _____

_____
_____
_____
_____
_____
_____
_____
_____
_____
_____
_____
_____
_____
_____
_____
_____
_____
_____
_____
_____
_____
_____
_____
_____
_____
_____

Notes:

Project Four

Variable Costing Versus Absorption Costing

Competencies

- Integrate *Microsoft® Excel* and *Microsoft® PowerPoint* to create a presentation that compares and contrasts variable costing and absorption costing.
- Explain how the variable-costing and absorption-costing methods influence the relationship between fixed costs and finished goods inventory.

Project Data

Sheet 1 is illustrated below:

	A	B	C	D	E	F	G
1							
2		**Variable-Costing**			**Absorption-Costing**		
3		**Income Statement**			**Income Statement**		
4							
5		Sales revenue............	$900,000		Sales revenue..........	$900,000	
6		Variable expenses......	540,000		Cost of goods sold......	450,000	
7							
8		Contribution margin...	$360,000		Gross margin...........	$450,000	
9		Fixed expenses.........	275,000		Operating expenses....	365,000	
10							
11		Net income...............	$85,000		Net income............	$85,000	
12							

Sheet 2 is illustrated below:

	A	B	C	D	E	F	G
1							
2		**Variable-Costing**			**Absorption-Costing**		
3		**Income Statement**			**Income Statement**		
4							
5		Sales revenue............	$890,000		Sales revenue............	$890,000	
6		Variable expenses......	537,000		Cost of goods sold......	445,000	
7							
8		Contribution margin...	$353,000		Gross margin............	$445,000	
9		Fixed expenses.........	275,000		Operating expenses...	365,000	
10							
11		Net income...............	$78,000		Net income...............	$80,000	
12							

An exhibit of slide 1 and an outline for the seven remaining slides of a presentation follows:

Title

44 pt.

Variable Costing Versus
Absorption Costing

Sub-title

32 pt.

By
Student's Name

Slide 2.　　　Title: Topics for Demonstration
　　　Bulleted list: Similarities between variable costing and absorption costing
　　　　　　　　Differences between variable costing and absorption costing

Slide 3.　　　Title: Two Definitions
　　　Bulleted list: Variable costing is assigning costs by their behavior
　　　　　　　　Absorption costing is assigning costs by their function

Slide 4.　　　Title: Two More Definitions
　　　Bulleted list: Contribution margin is the difference between sales revenue and
　　　　　　　　　variable costs
　　　　　　　　Gross margin is the difference between sales revenue and cost of
　　　　　　　　　goods sold

Slide 5.　　　Title: Equal Revenues, Equal Profits

　　　　　　　Note: Sheet 1 is pasted onto slide 5.

Slide 6.　　　Title: Equal Revenues, Unequal Profits

　　　　　　　Note: Sheet 2 is pasted onto slide 6

Slide 7.   Title: Conclusion
        Bulleted list: Variable costing and absorption costing can yield equal profits
                       Variable costing and absorption costing can yield unequal profits

Slide 8.   Title: That's All, Folks!

The speech text (partially completed) is as follows:

1. Ladies and Gentlemen: My name is Student's Name. Today, I am going to compare and contrast variable costing and absorption costing.

2. This means that I am going to demonstrate the similarities and differences—at least as far as income statements are concerned. When I demonstrate the similarities, I will show you income statements with equal profits. When I demonstrate the differences, I will show you income statements with unequal profits. Before I demonstrate the similarities and differences, however, I need to share four definitions with you.

3. First, variable costing is…[paraphrase the definition]. Second, absorption costing is…[paraphrase the definition].

4. Third, contribution margin is…[paraphrase the definition]. Fourth, gross margin (or gross profit) is…[paraphrase the definition].

5. The two costing methods can yield income statements with equal revenues and equal profits. Notice that these statements show revenues in the amount of $900,000. They also show profits in the amount of $85,000. This can happen if…[explain].

6. The two costing methods can yield income statements with equal revenues and unequal profits. Notice that these statements show revenues in the amount of $890,000. The profits, however, are different. [Indicate the amounts of profit and the reasons why.]

7. In conclusion…[focus on the relationship between fixed costs and finished goods inventory].

8. Thanks for your attention. Do you have any questions?

Required

1. Open *Excel* and create the two worksheets illustrated. Enter and format the numbers as shown. Use *Times New Roman* as a type font for all words and numbers. Use a bold type face.
2. Apply borders. The border should be around cell range A1 – G12 in each worksheet.
3. Apply colors. The fill color should be yellow. The font color should be blue.
4. Open *PowerPoint* and create a *title slide* using the data in the exhibit.
5. Apply a slide color scheme with a blue background.
6. Insert a *bulleted list* format for slides 2 – 4.
7. Insert a *title only* format for slide 5. Insert Sheet 1, cell range A1 – G12, onto this slide.
8. Insert a *title only* format for slide 6. Insert Sheet 2, cell range A1 – G12, onto this slide.
9. Insert a *bulleted list* format for slide 7.
10. Insert a *title only* format for slide 8.
11. Apply *dissolve* as a slide transition effect for slides 2 – 8.
12. Apply *fly from bottom* as text preset animation for slides 2 – 4 and 7.
13. Apply *speech text* to slides 1 – 8. Use information from Chapter M4 in the textbook to complete the speech.
14. Insert footers on the notes pages.
15. Save your project to a floppy disk.
16. Print the presentation as *notes pages*.
17. Staple the Transmittal Sheet on top of the notes pages.
18. On the Transmittal Sheet, explain how the variable-costing and absorption-costing methods influence the relationship between fixed costs and finished goods inventory.

Project Four Transmittal Sheet

Student Name: _____

Student Identification Number: _____

Class: _____

Date: _____

_____
_____
_____
_____
_____
_____
_____
_____
_____
_____
_____
_____
_____
_____
_____
_____
_____
_____
_____
_____
_____
_____
_____
_____

Notes:

Project Five

Activity-Based Costing

Competencies

- Integrate *Microsoft® Excel* and *Microsoft® Word* to create a report that explains and illustrates an activity-based costing budget.
- Show what happens to unit selling prices when overhead costs are changed.

Project Data

Report—Complete the document before inserting the worksheet cell ranges:

Activity-Based Costing Budget

By

Student's Name

This report explains and illustrates the activity-based costing (ABC) budget for Student's Name Corporation. Activity-based costing is…[paraphrase the textbook definition]. An ABC budget contains…[name the major sections of the budget].

The data section in the ABC budget contains four activity categories. The first activity category describes unit-level cost data. The costs that are bundled together in this category are…[describe the costs]. These costs total…[indicate the dollar amount].

[Insert Sheet 1, cell range A1 – H24, *as a picture*]

The second activity category describes batch-level costs. The overhead costs that are bundled in this category are…[describe the costs]. These costs total…[indicate the dollar amount].

The third activity category describes product-level costs. The only overhead costs in this category are…[describe the costs]. These costs total…[indicate the dollar amount].

The fourth activity category has to do with the manufacturing facility as a whole. Factory supervision in the amount of $99,000 is the overhead cost in this category.

The data section of the ABC budget also contains cost drivers and other product data. The first cost driver is the number of machine hours. Machine hours are matched with unit-level costs. Unit-level costs change as machine hours change.

The second cost driver is…[name, indicate how used].

The third cost driver is…[name, indicate how used].

There is no specific cost driver for facility-level costs. These costs cannot be associated directly with the products manufactured.

In the overhead cost calculations section of the ABC budget, overhead costs are allocated using cost drivers. First, unit-level overhead costs are matched with machine hours. For example, the unit-level overhead costs in cell C27 equal $74,880. That amount is equal to $187,200 times 4,000 machine hours divided by 10,000 machine hours.

[Insert Sheet 1, cell range A24 – H35, *as a picture*]

Second, batch-level overhead costs are matched with the number of batches. For example, the batch-level costs in cell C28 equal…[indicate the dollar amount]. The amount is equal to…[describe using numbers].

Third, product-level overhead costs are matched with extra inspections. These costs are allocated to the silver and gold widgets only.

Overhead costs to date are equal to the sum of the unit-level costs, batch-level costs, and product-level costs. Student's Name Corporation then allocates facility-level costs to the four products in proportion to the other overhead costs. For example, the $31,276 in cell C32 is equal to…[describe using numbers]. Total overhead costs are equal to overhead costs to date plus facility-level costs.

In the product unit calculations section of the ABC budget, unit costs and selling prices are determined for the widgets. The overhead cost per unit is equal to total overhead costs divided by the units of production. For example, the $0.47 in cell C38 is equal to…[describe using numbers].

[Insert Sheet 1, cell range A35 – H48, *as a picture*]

Total cost per unit equals the overhead cost per unit plus the direct materials cost per unit plus the direct labor cost per unit. For example, the total cost in cell C42 is…[indicate amount]. It is equal to…[explain using numbers].

The selling price per unit is equal to the total cost per unit times 160%. The selling price of the gold widgets is significantly higher because the overhead and direct materials costs are significantly higher.

The gross profit per unit is equal to the selling price per unit minus the total cost per unit. The gross profit percentage is…[explain].

Student's Name Corporation uses activity-based costing because...[enter your reasons here].

Sheet 1: ABC Budget
The formula in cell C27 is =SUM(C7:C10)*C17/SUM(C17:F17)
The formula in cell C32 is =G13*C31/G31

	A	B	C	D	E	F	G	H
1								
2		STUDENT'S NAME CORPORATION						
3		ACTIVITY-BASED COSTING BUDGET						
4		YEAR ENDED DECEMBER 31, THIS YEAR						
5								
6		Unit-level cost data			Batch-level cost data			
7		Factory depreciation	$112,000		Machine setups		$120,000	
8		Packaging and shipping	54,000		Materials handling		91,800	
9		Factory utilities	14,000		Standard inspections		84,000	
10		Repairs and maintenance	7,200					
11								
12		Product-level cost data			Facility-level cost data			
13		Extra inspections	$12,000		Factory supervision		$99,000	
14								
15		Cost drivers and product data	Black	Blue	Silver	Gold	All	
16			Widgets	Widgets	Widgets	Widgets	Widgets	
17		Machine hours	4,000	3,000	2,000	1,000		
18		Batches	16	12	10	20		
19		Extra inspections	0	0	10	20		
20		Units of production	400,000	300,000	200,000	100,000		
21		Direct materials cost per unit	$0.10	$0.10	$0.16	$0.20		
22		Direct labor cost per unit	$0.24	$0.24	$0.24	$0.24		
23		Cost to selling price markup percent					160%	
24								
25		Overhead cost calculations	Black	Blue	Silver	Gold		
26			Widgets	Widgets	Widgets	Widgets	Total	
27		Unit-level costs (machine hours)	$74,880	$56,160	$37,440	$18,720	$187,200	
28		Batch-level costs (batches)	81,600	61,200	51,000	102,000	295,800	
29		Product-level costs (extra inspections)	0	0	4,000	8,000	12,000	
30								
31		Overhead costs to date	$156,480	$117,360	$92,440	$128,720	$495,000	
32		Facility-level costs (OH costs to date)	31,296	23,472	18,488	25,744	99,000	
33								
34		Total overhead costs	$187,776	$140,832	$110,928	$154,464	$594,000	
35								
36		Product unit calculations	Black	Blue	Silver	Gold		
37			Widgets	Widgets	Widgets	Widgets		
38		Overhead cost per unit	$0.47	$0.47	$0.55	$1.54		
39		Direct materials cost per unit	0.10	0.10	0.16	0.20		
40		Direct labor cost per unit	0.24	0.24	0.24	0.24		
41								
42		Total cost per unit	$0.81	$0.81	$0.95	$1.98		
43		Selling price per unit	1.30	1.30	1.53	3.18		
44								
45		Gross profit per unit	$0.49	$0.49	$0.57	$1.19		
46		Gross profit percentage	37.50%	37.50%	37.50%	37.50%		
47								
48		Project 5, Student's Name, Identification Number, Class Number, Today's Date						

Required

1. <u>Open</u> *Word* and format a new document. Enter the report as shown above. Refer to Chapter M5 in the textbook for information to complete your report.
2. <u>Open</u> *Excel* and create the worksheet that is illustrated on pages 5.3 and 5.4. <u>Merge</u> and center text in rows 2 – 4 and in the bottom row. <u>Enter</u> cell-based formulas and functions for all calculations. Create some formulas based upon information in the report that you typed. Create other formulas based upon information in Chapter M5 of the textbook. <u>Format</u> all numbers as shown.
3. <u>Format</u> the *Excel* worksheet to show gridlines. Make sure that the worksheet is also formatted to show row and column headings.
4. <u>Insert</u> the *Excel* worksheet cell ranges *as pictures* into the *Word* document where indicated.
5. <u>Insert</u> footers into the *Word* document.
6. <u>Save</u> your project to a floppy disk.
7. <u>Print</u> the *Word* document (your report).
8. <u>Staple</u> the Transmittal Sheet on top of the document.
9. <u>Copy</u> the worksheets.
10. <u>Print</u> each worksheet copy to show the formulas.
11. <u>Staple</u> the worksheet copies to the back of the Transmittal Sheet following the report.
12. On the Transmittal Sheet, show what happens to the unit selling prices when the facility-level (overhead) costs are doubled. Change the Sheet 1 data in cell G13 to get the revised unit selling prices in row 43. Use the format below:

Product unit calculations	Black Widgets	Blue Widgets	Silver Widgets	Gold Widgets
Selling price per unit when facility-level costs are doubled				
Original selling price per unit				
Increase in selling price per unit				

Project Five Transmittal Sheet

Student Name: _____

Student Identification Number: _____

Class: _____

Date: _____

_____
_____
_____
_____
_____
_____
_____
_____
_____
_____
_____
_____
_____
_____
_____
_____
_____
_____
_____
_____
_____
_____
_____
_____
_____

Notes:

Project Six

The Master Budget

Competencies

- Use *Microsoft® Excel* to create and describe a collection of related budgets in a master budget workbook.
- Create a pro forma budgeted balance sheet based upon information in a master budget workbook.

Project Data

Sheet 1. Budget data—upper section

	B	C	D	E	F
1					
2	STUDENT'S NAME CORPORATION				
3	THE MASTER BUDGET				
4	YEAR ENDED DECEMBER 31, THIS YEAR				
5					
6	DATA IN DOLLARS:	1st Qtr	2nd Qtr	3rd Qtr	4th Qtr
7					
8	Accounts payable, prior year ending balance..................	$26,000			
9	Accounts receivable, prior year ending balance..............	90,000			
10	Accumulated depreciation, prior year end. balance.........	290,000			
11	Borrowings, beginning of quarter....................................	100,000	$40,000	$0	$0
12	Building and equipment, prior year ending balance.........	600,000			
13	Cash dividends paid...	10,000	10,000	10,000	10,000
14	Cash, prior year ending balance....................................	74,000			
15	Common stock, prior year ending balance......................	180,000			
16	Direct labor cost per hour..	10.00	10.00	10.00	10.00
17	Direct materials cost per pound.....................................	0.60	0.60	0.60	0.60
18	Equipment purchases..	20,000	20,000	40,000	40,000
19	Income taxes payable, prior year ending balance...........	60,000			
20	Interest payments, end of quarter..................................	2,500	3,500	3,500	1,500
21	Land, prior year ending balance....................................	75,000			
22	Overhead, depreciation..	12,000	12,000	12,000	12,000
23	Overhead, fixed...	60,000	60,000	60,000	60,000
24	Overhead, variable rate per hour...................................	2.00	2.00	2.00	2.00
25	Principle payments, end of quarter................................	0	0	80,000	0
26	Retained earnings, prior year ending balance...............	389,034			
27	Selling and admin. exp., variable cost per unit..............	1.86	1.86	1.86	1.86
28	Selling and administrative fixed expenses:				
29	Advertising...	22,000	22,000	22,000	22,000
30	Executive salaries..	56,000	56,000	56,000	56,000
31	Insurance..	10,000	10,000	10,000	10,000
32	Property taxes...	4,500	4,500	4,500	4,500
33	Depreciation...	8,000	8,000	8,000	8,000
34	Selling price per unit..	24.50	24.50	24.50	24.50
35					

Sheet 1. Budget data—lower section

	A	B	C	D	E	F	G
35							
36		DATA IN HOURS:	1st Qtr	2nd Qtr	3rd Qtr	4th Qtr	
37							
38		Direct labor hours per unit..	0.75	0.75	0.75	0.75	
39							
40		DATA IN PERCENTAGES:	1st Qtr	2nd Qtr	3rd Qtr	4th Qtr	
41							
42		Federal and state income tax rate............................	40%	40%	40%	40%	
43		Cash collection in quarter of sale................................	70%	70%	70%	70%	
44		Cash collection in quarter following sale.......................	30%	30%	30%	30%	
45		Cash payment in quarter of purchase..........................	60%	60%	60%	60%	
46		Cash payment in quarter following purchase.................	40%	40%	40%	40%	
47							
48		DATA IN UNITS:	1st Qtr	2nd Qtr	3rd Qtr	4th Qtr	
49							
50		Direct materials, pounds required per widget..................	10	10	10	10	
51		Direct materials, beginning inventory in pounds..............	20,000	34,000	36,000	25,000	
52		Direct materials, ending inventory in pounds..................	34,000	36,000	25,000	24,000	
53		Finished goods, beginning inventory in units.................	2,000	6,000	8,000	4,000	
54		Finished goods, ending inventory in units....................	6,000	8,000	4,000	3,000	
55		Finished goods, sales in units.....................................	20,000	32,000	40,000	26,000	
56							
57		Project 6, Student's Name, Identification Number, Class Number, Today's Date					

Sheet 2. Budget calculations—upper section

	A	B	C	D	E	F	G	H
1								
2		STUDENT'S NAME CORPORATION						
3		THE MASTER BUDGET						
4		YEAR ENDED DECEMBER 31, THIS YEAR						
5								
6		SALES BUDGET	1st Qtr	2nd Qtr	3rd Qtr	4th Qtr	Year	
7		Expected sales revenue...	$490,000	$784,000	$980,000	$637,000	$2,891,000	
8		The sales budget projects revenue from our company's products. It is based upon marketing department forecasts.						
9								
10		CASH COLLECTIONS SCHEDULE	1st Qtr	2nd Qtr	3rd Qtr	4th Qtr	Year	
11		Expected cash collections...	$433,000	$695,800	$921,200	$739,900	$2,789,900	
12		The cash collections schedule projects future collections based upon past experience in Accounts Receivable.						
13								
14		PRODUCTION BUDGET	1st Qtr	2nd Qtr	3rd Qtr	4th Qtr	Year	
15		Expected sales in units..	20,000	32,000	40,000	26,000	118,000	
16		Add finished goods end. inv.......................................	6,000	8,000	4,000	3,000	3,000	
17								
18		Total units required...	26,000	40,000	44,000	29,000	121,000	
19		Less finished goods beg. inventory.............................	2,000	6,000	8,000	4,000	2,000	
20								
21		Units to be produced...	24,000	34,000	36,000	25,000	119,000	
22		The production budget identifies the number of widgets to be produced to satisfy sales and inventory needs.						
23								

Sheet2: Budget calculations—lower section

	A	B	C	D	E	F	G	H
23								
24		**DIRECT MATERIALS BUDGET**	**1st Qtr**	**2nd Qtr**	**3rd Qtr**	**4th Qtr**	**Year**	
25		Direct materials needed for production............................	240,000	340,000	360,000	250,000	1,190,000	
26		Add direct materials ending inventory..............................	34,000	36,000	25,000	24,000	24,000	
27								
28		Total direct materials required.......................................	274,000	376,000	385,000	274,000	1,214,000	
29		Less direct materials beg. inventory...............................	20,000	34,000	36,000	25,000	20,000	
30								
31		Direct materials to be purchased....................................	254,000	342,000	349,000	249,000	1,194,000	
32								
33		Expected cost of direct materials...................................	$152,400	$205,200	$209,400	$149,400	$716,400	
34		The direct materials budget identifies the units of materials needed to support our company's widget production.						
35								
36		**CASH PAYMENTS FOR DIRECT MATERIALS**	**1st Qtr**	**2nd Qtr**	**3rd Qtr**	**4th Qtr**	**Year**	
37		Payment of accounts payable, beg. balance....................	$26,000				$26,000	
38		Payment of lst quarter purchases...................................	91,440	$60,960			152,400	
39		Payment of 2nd quarter purchases.................................		123,120	$82,080		205,200	
40		Payment of 3rd quarter purchases..................................			125,640	$83,760	209,400	
41		Payment of 4th quarter purchases..................................				89,640	89,640	
42								
43		Total cash payments for direct materials.........................	$117,440	$184,080	$207,720	$173,400	$682,640	
44		Cash payments for direct materials are actually payments on account (Accounts Payable).						
45								
46		**DIRECT LABOR BUDGET**	**1st Qtr**	**2nd Qtr**	**3rd Qtr**	**4th Qtr**	**Year**	
47		Direct labor hours planned..	18,000	25,500	27,000	18,750	89,250	
48								
49		Cash payments for direct labor.......................................	$180,000	$255,000	$270,000	$187,500	$892,500	
50		The direct labor budget identifies the cost of human resources needed to meet our company's widget production.						
51								
52		**MANUFACTURING OVERHEAD BUDGET**	**1st Qtr**	**2nd Qtr**	**3rd Qtr**	**4th Qtr**	**Year**	
53		Variable manufacturing overhead....................................	$36,000	$51,000	$54,000	$37,500	$178,500	
54		Fixed manufacturing overhead..	60,000	60,000	60,000	60,000	240,000	
55								
56		Total manufacturing overhead..	96,000	111,000	114,000	97,500	418,500	
57		Less factory depreciation..	12,000	12,000	12,000	12,000	48,000	
58								
59		Cash payments for overhead..	$84,000	$99,000	$102,000	$85,500	$370,500	
60		The manufacturing overhead budget projects all costs of production other than direct materials and direct labor.						
61								
62		Project 6, Student's Name, Identification Number, Class Number, Today's Date						

Sheet 3: Budget calculations—upper section

	A	B	C	D	E	F	G	H
1								
2		**STUDENT'S NAME CORPORATION**						
3		**THE MASTER BUDGET**						
4		**YEAR ENDED DECEMBER 31, THIS YEAR**						
5								
6		**FINISHED GOODS UNIT COST**	**1st Qtr**	**2nd Qtr**	**3rd Qtr**	**4th Qtr**		
7		Direct materials cost per unit..	$6.00	$6.00	$6.00	$6.00		
8		Direct labor cost per unit..	7.50	7.50	7.50	7.50		
9		Manufacturing overhead cost per unit.............................	3.52	3.52	3.52	3.52		
10								
11		Total cost per unit...	$17.02	$17.02	$17.02	$17.02		
12		The manufacturing overhead cost per unit equals manufacturing overhead for the year divided by annual production.						
13								

Sheet 3: Budget calculations—lower section

	A	B	C	D	E	F	G	H
13								
14		SELLING AND ADMIN. EXPENSE BUDGET	1st Qtr	2nd Qtr	3rd Qtr	4th Qtr	Year	
15		Budgeted variable expense............................	$37,200	$59,520	$74,400	$48,360	$219,480	
16		Budgeted fixed expenses:						
17		Advertising.........................	22,000	22,000	22,000	22,000	88,000	
18		Executive salaries..................	56,000	56,000	56,000	56,000	224,000	
19		Insurance...........................	10,000	10,000	10,000	10,000	40,000	
20		Property taxes......................	4,500	4,500	4,500	4,500	18,000	
21		Depreciation.......................	8,000	8,000	8,000	8,000	32,000	
22								
23		Total selling and administrative expenses............	137,700	160,020	174,900	148,860	621,480	
24		Less depreciation expense......................	8,000	8,000	8,000	8,000	32,000	
25		Cash payments for selling and						
26		administrative expenses....................	$129,700	$152,020	$166,900	$140,860	$589,480	
27		The selling and administrative expense budget contains projected expenses for nonmanufacturing activities.						
28								
29		PRO FORMA INCOME STATEMENT	1st Qtr	2nd Qtr	3rd Qtr	4th Qtr	Year	
30		Sales revenue..........................	$490,000	$784,000	$980,000	$637,000	$2,891,000	
31		Less cost of goods sold.....................	340,336	544,538	680,672	442,437	2,007,983	
32								
33		Gross margin........................	149,664	239,462	299,328	194,563	883,017	
34		Less selling and administrative..............	137,700	160,020	174,900	148,860	621,480	
35								
36		Net operating income (loss).................	11,964	79,442	124,428	45,703	261,537	
37		Less interest expense.....................	2,500	3,500	3,500	1,500	11,000	
38		Less income taxes expense.................	3,786	30,377	48,371	17,681	100,215	
39								
40		Net income (loss).....................	$5,678	$45,565	$72,557	$26,522	$150,322	
41		The income statement is called pro forma because it is a budget instead of the results of actual operations.						
42								
43		CASH BUDGET	1st Qtr	2nd Qtr	3rd Qtr	4th Qtr	Year	
44		Cash in bank, beginning of quarter.............	$74,000	$3,360	$11,774	$22,478	$74,000	
45		Expected collections from customers.............	433,000	695,800	921,200	739,900	2,789,900	
46		Payments:						
47		Direct materials........................	117,440	184,080	207,720	173,400	682,640	
48		Direct labor.........................	180,000	255,000	270,000	187,500	892,500	
49		Manufacturing overhead.................	84,000	99,000	102,000	85,500	370,500	
50		Selling and administrative...............	129,700	152,020	166,900	140,860	589,480	
51		Equipment purchases..................	20,000	20,000	40,000	40,000	120,000	
52		Dividends.........................	10,000	10,000	10,000	10,000	40,000	
53		Income tax.........................	60,000	3,786	30,377	48,371	142,534	
54								
55		Total payments........................	601,140	723,886	826,997	685,631	2,837,654	
56		Excess (deficiency) of cash before						
57		financing..........................	(94,140)	(24,726)	105,978	76,746	26,246	
58		Financing:						
59		Borrowings, beginning of quarter.............	100,000	40,000	0	0	140,000	
60		Less principle payments, end of quarter.........	0	0	80,000	0	80,000	
61		Less interest payments, end of quarter.........	2,500	3,500	3,500	1,500	11,000	
62								
63		Total financing increase (decrease).............	97,500	36,500	(83,500)	(1,500)	49,000	
64								
65		Cash in bank, end of quarter...............	$3,360	$11,774	$22,478	$75,246	$75,246	
66		The cash budget describes the cash requirements for each quarter and the year as a whole.						
67								
68		Project 6, Student's Name, Identification Number, Class Number, Today's Date						

-6.4-

Format of pro forma balance sheet

STUDENT'S NAME CORPORATION
PRO FORMA BALANCE SHEET
DECEMBER 31, THIS YEAR

ASSETS

Cash.. $

Accounts receivable.....................................

Direct materials inventory.............................

Finished goods inventory..............................

Land..

Buildings and equipment..............................

Accumulated depreciation............................

Total assets... $

LIABILITIES AND STOCKHOLDERS' EQUITY

Accounts payable.. $

Income taxes payable.................................

Common stock...

Retained earnings.......................................

Total liabilities and stockholders' equity........... $

Required

Make sure that you complete the following steps in order. Refer to the procedures in the Appendix, which are alphabetized by underlined verb. Note the underlined verbs in the steps below.

1. <u>Open</u> *Excel* and create three worksheets to look like the examples in the project. <u>Merge</u> and center the text in rows 2 – 4 and in the bottom row of each worksheet. <u>Enter</u> cell-based formulas and functions to calculate all amounts in worksheets 2 and 3. The exhibits in Chapter M6 of the textbook will add to your understanding of the worksheet budgets.
2. <u>Format</u> each worksheet. Do not select gridlines.
3. <u>Save</u> your project to a floppy disk.

4. Review the worksheets and make the following data changes on Sheet 1:

   Change the cash dividends paid to $8,000 each quarter
   Change the direct materials cost per pound to $0.61 each quarter
   Change the executive salaries to $57,000 each quarter

5. Print the workbook after the above changes are made.
6. Staple the worksheets to the back of the Transmittal Sheet.
6. Copy Sheet 2 and Sheet 3.
7. Print each worksheet copy to show the formulas.
8. Staple the worksheet copies to the back of the Transmittal Sheet behind the worksheets printed in step 5.
9. Create by hand a pro forma balance sheet on the Transmittal Sheet. Use the example shown on page 6.5. Enter the account balances rounded to the nearest dollar. Chapter M6 of the textbook shows how to get the account balances. The amount for total assets equals $755,272. Adjust retained earnings so that the total liabilities and stockholders' equity amount also equals $755,272.

Project Six Transmittal Sheet

Student Name: _____

Student Identification Number: _____

Class: _____

Date: _____

_____
_____
_____
_____
_____
_____
_____
_____
_____
_____
_____
_____
_____
_____
_____
_____
_____
_____
_____
_____
_____
_____
_____
_____
_____
_____
_____

Notes:

Project Seven

Variance Analysis

Competencies

- Integrate *Microsoft*® *Excel* and *Microsoft*® *Word* to create and describe variance analysis of variable manufacturing costs.
- Apply what-if analysis of three scenarios using a variance-analysis worksheet.

Project Data

Sheet 1. Upper section

	A	B	C	D	E	F
1						
2		STUDENT'S NAME CORPORATION				
3		VARIANCE ANALYSIS OF VARIABLE COSTS				
4		MONTH ENDED JANUARY 31, THIS YEAR				
5						
6		PRODUCTION DATA			Total	
7		Number of widgets produced..			1,800	
8						
9		STANDARD COST DATA PER UNIT OF OUTPUT	Unit	Unit	Unit	
10			Description	Quantity	Price	
11		Direct materials...	pounds	8	$0.55	
12		Direct labor..	labor hours	2.2	10.00	
13		Variable manufacturing overhead......................	machine hours	4.4	3.00	
14						
15		ACTUAL COST DATA FOR THE MONTH	Unit	Unit	Unit	
16			Description	Quantity	Price	
17		Direct materials used in production........................	pounds	14,000	$0.60	
18		Direct labor..	labor hours	4,000	10.25	
19		Variable manufacturing overhead......................	machine hours	8,000	2.90	
20						
21		CALCULATION OF MATERIALS COSTS			Total	
22		Actual quantity of direct materials at actual unit price..			$8,400	
23		Actual quantity of direct materials at standard unit price..............................			7,700	
24		Standard quantity of direct materials at standard unit price.............................			7,920	
25						
26		CALCULATION OF MATERIALS VARIANCES			Unfavorable	
27					(Favorable)	
28		Price variance..			$700	
29		Quantity variance...			(220)	
30						
31		Total materials variance..			$480	
32						

Sheet 1. Lower section

	A	B	C	D	E	F
32						
33		CALCULATION OF LABOR COSTS			Total	
34		Actual hours of labor at actual rate per hour..			$41,000	
35		Actual hours of labor at standard rate per hour..			40,000	
36		Standard hours of labor at standard rate per hour...			39,600	
37						
38		CALCULATION OF LABOR VARIANCES			Unfavorable	
39					(Favorable)	
40		Rate variance..			$1,000	
41		Efficiency variance...			400	
42						
43		Total labor variance..			$1,400	
44						
45		CALCULATION OF VARIABLE OVERHEAD COSTS			Total	
46		Actual machine hours at the actual rate per hour...			$23,200	
47		Actual machine hours at the standard rate per hour..			24,000	
48		Standard machine hours at the standard rate per hour.....................................			23,760	
49						
50		CALCULATION OF VARIABLE OVERHEAD VARIANCES			Unfavorable	
51					(Favorable)	
52		Spending variance...			($800)	
53		Efficiency variance...			240	
54						
55		Total variable overhead variance..			($560)	
56						
57		Project 7, Student's Name, Identification Number, Class Number, Today's Date				

Notes about variance analysis

1. Standard costs are budgeted costs of manufacturing. They are predetermined. They represent what the costs of direct materials, labor, and variable overhead should be for the number of widgets actually produced.
2. Standard costs come from the engineering department. Their studies are the source of pounds, labor hours, and machine hours, as well as unit costs.
3. Variance analysis is the calculation and interpretation of the differences between standard costs and actual costs. Favorable variances, negative amounts, mean Student's Name Corporation is saving money. Unfavorable variances, positive amounts, mean the corporation is spending more than expected.
4. There are two components of direct materials variance used by Student's Name Corporation—price and quantity. The corporation also uses two components of labor variance—rate and efficiency. The calculations are shown in Chapter M7 of the textbook.
5. There are also two components of variable overhead variance—spending and efficiency. In Student's Name Corporation the spending variance in cell E52 = E46 – E47. The efficiency variance in cell E53 = E47 – E48.
6. Student's Name Corporation does no variance analysis for fixed overhead costs. Fixed costs are not supposed to change.

Required

1. Open *Excel* according to the procedures in Appendix A. Merge and center the text in rows 2 – 4 and 57. Create a worksheet like the example in this project. Enter a cell-based formula to calculate each variance. Information in Chapter M7 of the textbook will help your understanding of the variances. Format the worksheet. Do not use gridlines.
2. Open *Word* and create a report from the notes provided. The report title should be *Variance Analysis of Variable Costs by Student's Name*. The report should be for new personnel so that they will understand how variance analysis is used in Student's Name Corporation. Make sure that your document has an introduction, main body, and conclusion. Insert the following cell ranges of the *Excel* worksheet *as pictures* into your *Word* document:

    A1 – F20 when you discuss standard cost data and actual cost data
    A20 – F32 when you discuss calculation of materials costs and variances
    A32 – F44 when you discuss calculation of labor costs and variances
    A44 – F57 when you discuss calculation of overhead costs and variances

3. Insert footers into your document.
4. Save your project to a floppy disk.
5. On the Transmittal Sheet, create the following table by hand. Record the variances for the three different quantities of widgets. Assume that the actual cost data remains the same. What conclusion can be reached? Is this an appropriate conclusion?

Number of widgets produced	1,800	1,850	1,900
	Unfavorable	Unfavorable	Unfavorable
Calculation of variances	(Favorable)	(Favorable)	(Favorable)
Total materials variance	$480		
Total labor variance	$1,400		
Total variable overhead variance	($560)		

6. Copy the worksheet.
7. Print the worksheet copy to show the formulas.
8. Staple the Transmittal Sheet on top of your report.

Project Seven Transmittal Sheet

Student Name: _____

Student Identification Number: _____

Class: _____

Date: _____

_____
_____
_____
_____
_____
_____
_____
_____
_____
_____
_____
_____
_____
_____
_____
_____
_____
_____
_____
_____
_____
_____
_____
_____
_____

Notes:

Project Eight

Performance Evaluation

Competencies

- Integrate *Microsoft® Excel* and *Microsoft® Word* to create a report that describes measures used to evaluate the performance of two production departments.
- Apply what-if analysis at different levels of sales revenue using the performance evaluation worksheet.

Project Data

Sheet 1. Data and calculations

	A	B	C	D	E	F
1						
2		STUDENT'S NAME CORPORATION				
3		PERFORMANCE EVALUATION				
4		YEAR ENDED DECEMBER 31, THIS YEAR				
5						
6			STANDARD	CUSTOM		
7			WIDGET	WIDGET		
8		DATA	DEPARTMENT	DEPARTMENT	TOTAL	
9						
10		Average operating assets.........................	$300,000,000	$375,000,000		
11		Net sales..	850,000,000	750,000,000		
12		Cost-of-goods-sold percentages..................	80%	75%		
13		Operating expenses................................			$198,000,000	
14						
15		CALCULATIONS				
16		Revenue:				
17		Net sales..	$850,000,000	$750,000,000	$1,600,000,000	
18		Expenses:				
19		Cost of goods sold...................................	680,000,000	562,500,000	1,242,500,000	
20		Operating expenses.................................	105,187,500	92,812,500	198,000,000	
21						
22		Operating income.....................................	$64,812,500	$94,687,500	$159,500,000	
23						
24		Margin..	7.63%	12.63%		
25		Turnover..	2.83	2.00		
26		Return on investment.................................	21.60%	25.25%		
27						
28		Project 8, Student's Name, Identification Number, Class Number, Today's Date				

Notes about the performance-evaluation worksheet

1. Average operating assets = (Asset balance at last year end + asset balance at this year end) / 2. Operating assets are limited to those assets controlled by each department in this company. The assets include cash, accounts receivable, inventories, and the plant assets used for manufacturing the widgets. The departments are cost centers.
2. Net sales is the total selling price of all widgets sold to customers during the year less any returns.
3. The cost-of-goods-sold percentages are 80% for the standard widget department and 75% for the custom widget department. The higher percentage for the standard widget department is due to competition. Cost of goods sold includes direct materials, direct labor, and manufacturing overhead. Activity-based costing is used to allocate manufacturing overhead costs.
4. Total operating expenses include selling and administrative costs, but do not include interest and taxes. Operating expenses are allocated to the departments in proportion to sales revenue generated. The company does not use activity-based costing for these expenses.
5. Operating income = sales revenue − (cost of goods + operating expenses). In this company, operating income can also be called earnings before interest and taxes (EBIT). Operating income is not the same as net income.
6. Margin = operating income / sales revenue. Margin is also known as operating-income percentage. The margin is lower for the standard widget department than for the custom widget department because the cost of goods sold percentage is higher.
7. Turnover = sales revenue / average operating assets. It is expressed as the number of times per year inventory turns over. The turnover is lower in the custom widget department because computer-integrated manufacturing equipment is used to reduce cycle time in that department. This higher priced equipment has not yet been purchased for the standard widget department.
8. Return on investment = operating income / average operating assets. Also, return on investment = margin * turnover. It is expressed as a percentage of average operating assets. The minimum return on investment (ROI) for each department is 18%.

Required

Make sure that you complete the following steps in order. Refer to the procedures in the Appendix, which are alphabetized by underlined verb. Note the underlined verbs in the steps below.

1. Open *Excel* and create a worksheet like the example in this project. Merge and center the text in rows 2 – 4 and 28. Use cell-based formulas and functions for calculations in rows 17 – 26. Format the worksheet. Do not use gridlines.
2. Open *Word* and create a report from the notes provided and from the information in Chapter M9 of the textbook. Make sure that your document has an introduction, main

body, and conclusion. The report title should be *The Performance-Evaluation Worksheet by Student's Name.* Insert *Excel*, cell range A1 – F14, *as a picture* into the Word document. Explain the data. Insert *Excel*, cell range A14 – F28 *as a picture* into the *Word* document. Explain the calculations. Insert footers into your *Word* document. Your conclusion should include your opinion as to the fairness of this method of performance evaluation. The departments are cost centers.

3. Save your project to a floppy disk.
4. Print your Word document and attach it to the back of the Transmittal Sheet.
5. Copy the worksheet.
6. Print the worksheet copy in a format that shows the formulas and functions. Attach the worksheet copy to the back of the Transmittal Sheet behind the report.
7. Create the following table by hand on the Transmittal Sheet.

	STANDARD WIDGET DEPARTMENT	CUSTOM WIDGET DEPARTMENT
Net sales	$900,000,000	$900,000,000
Margin		
Turnover		
Return on investment		
Net sales	$900,000,000	$850,000,000
Margin		
Turnover		
Return on investment		
Net sales	$900,000,000	$800,000,000
Margin		
Turnover		
Return on investment		

8. Keep the sales for the standard widget department at $900,000,000. Enter the different sales amounts for the custom widget department in the data section of your original worksheet. Record the calculations for both departments on your Transmittal Sheet. Why might the manager of the standard widget department object to being evaluated based upon these performance measures? What recommendations do you have regarding how costs are allocated?

Project Eight Transmittal Sheet

Student Name: _____

Student Identification Number: _____

Class: _____

Date: _____

_____
_____
_____
_____
_____
_____
_____
_____
_____
_____
_____
_____
_____
_____
_____
_____
_____
_____
_____
_____
_____
_____
_____

Notes:

Project Nine

Just-In-Time Manufacturing System

Competencies

- Integrate *Microsoft® Excel* and *Microsoft® PowerPoint* to create a presentation that proposes the implementation of a just-in-time manufacturing system.
- Explain how a just-in-time manufacturing system can improve the return on assets when it is installed.

Project Data

A partially completed worksheet is illustrated below:

	WITHOUT JIT SYSTEM	WITH JIT SYSTEM
Expected sales revenue.............	$74,000,000	
Variable manufacturing costs...	29,600,000	
Fixed manufacturing costs......	28,000,000	
Fixed selling and admin. exp...	11,000,000	
Operating income..................	$5,400,000	
Average total assets...............	$140,000,000	
Return on assets....................	4%	

The following statistics are projected if the JIT manufacturing system is implemented:

> Sales revenue will increase 20% according to our marketing people.
> Variable manufacturing costs will decrease from 40% to 36% of sales revenue.
> Fixed manufacturing costs will decrease 25% according to our production people.
> Fixed sales and administration will decrease 15%.
> Average total assets will decrease 2% according to our controller.

Exhibits of the first slide and last slide are as follows:

Just-In-Time Manufacturing

A Proposal By
Student's Name

That's All, Folks!

Notes for the slide presentation are as follows:

If Student's Name Corporation implements a JIT system, the return on assets (19%) will be better than most companies in the industry.

Student's Name Corporation currently uses a push system—one that produces widgets based upon forecasts of market demand. Direct materials, component parts, or finished goods are stored just in case they might be needed. The return on assets (4%) is worse that most companies in the industry.

Required

1. <u>Open</u> *Excel* and create the worksheet illustrated. Use formulas to create the numbers in the *With JIT System* column. Use *Times New Roman* as a type font for all words and numbers. Format the numbers as shown. Use a yellow background and a blue font color. All letters and numbers should be bold. Do not set the worksheet up for printing.
2. <u>Open</u> *PowerPoint* and create a *title slide* using the data in the exhibit.
3. <u>Apply</u> a slide color scheme with a blue background.
4. <u>Insert</u> appropriate slides that will make your case to the board of directors for implementing a just-in-time manufacturing system. Include what the JIT system does; push system versus pull system, financial projections without or with JIT, advantages, disadvantages, and conclusions—risks and rewards. <u>Insert</u> the worksheet in one of the slides where appropriate. Refer to information in Chapter M9 of the textbook to make your case. End with the *That's all, folks* slide.
5. <u>Apply</u> *dissolve* as a slide transition effect for slides two through the last slide.
6. <u>Apply</u> *fly from bottom* as text preset animation where appropriate.
7. <u>Apply</u> *speech text* to the slides. Base your speech on information in Chapter M9 of the textbook and on the notes above.
8. <u>Insert</u> footers on to the notes pages.
9. <u>Save</u> your project to a floppy disk.
10. <u>Print</u> the slides as *notes pages* and attach them to the back of the Transmittal Sheet.
11. On the front of the Transmittal Sheet, explain how a just-in-time manufacturing system can improve the return on assets when it is installed.

Project Nine Transmittal Sheet

Student Name: _____

Student Identification Number: _____

Class: _____

Date: _____

_____
_____
_____
_____
_____
_____
_____
_____
_____
_____
_____
_____
_____
_____
_____
_____
_____
_____
_____
_____
_____
_____
_____
_____

Notes:

Project Ten

Capital Investment Decisions

Competencies

- Integrate *Microsoft® Excel* and *Microsoft® Word* to create a report that explains and demonstrates capital investment decisions using the following methods: net present value, internal rate of return, payback period, and accounting rate of return.
- Apply what-if analysis at different levels of sales revenue using a capital-investment-proposal worksheet.

Project Data

Notes about the capital-investment-proposal worksheet

1. Student's Name Corporation develops this worksheet to make capital investment decisions regarding a new factory for manufacturing widgets. In this proposal the factory building will be rented for four years with a four-year option to renew. The fixed assets (machinery, equipment, furniture, fixtures, and computer system) will be purchased without financing. A residual value for the fixed assets is not considered.

2. The expected life of the investment is four years, but the investment will be reevaluated for an additional four years during the fourth year. The computer system will probably have to be replaced at that time. A return of working capital at the end of four years is not considered because the lease will probably be renewed.

3. This proposal takes MACRS and federal and state income taxes into account. MACRS is an acronym for Modified Accelerated Cost Recovery System. It is the business asset depreciation system that is used on tax returns. Depreciation for a particular year is equal to the cost times the recovery year percentage. For example, the depreciation on the computer system for the first year = $600,000 X 20.00% = $120,000. The combined federal and state tax rate is assumed to be 40.00%.

4. All amounts in the calculation sections come from formulas or functions. The formulas and functions are particularly valuable for what-if analysis. When the data is changed for what-if analysis, the calculations automatically change the amounts shown. This proposal assumes that the annual revenue, cost of goods sold, and operating expenses (except depreciation) are the same for each of the five years.

5. The net present value is the difference between the present value of future cash inflows and the present value of expected cash outflows. It is assumed that total cash outflows for the investment are made today. For that reason, the present value of total cash outflows is equal to the investment. The present value of cash inflows in cell C39 is equal to the sum of the amounts in cells D39 through G39. The amounts in cells D39 through G39 are calculated using a present value (PV) function. For example, the present value in cell D39 is calculated as follows:

$$=-PV(C14,D19,0,D37)$$

Proposed investments are rejected when the net present value is negative. A negative number means that the proposed investment does not meet the required rate of return of 15%.

6. The internal rate of return is the interest rate that causes the present value of cash inflows to equal the cash outflows from the proposed investment. The rate in cell C16 is adjusted manually until the present value of cash inflows in cell C48 is equal to the total cash outflow in cell C45. The amount in cell C48 is equal to the sum of the amounts in cells D48 – G48. The amounts in cells D48 – G48 are calculated using a present value function. For example, the amount in cell D48 is calculated as follows:

$$=-PV(C16,D44,0,D46)$$

7. The payback period establishes when the original investment is recovered by expected future cash inflows. In this proposal the original investment is recovered during the third year. The cash inflows are not discounted to present value. The time value of money is ignored.

8. The accounting rate of return is the average income per year generated by this proposed project divided by the investment in the project. The interest rate is higher because it ignores the time value of money.

9. The residual values of the fixed assets are equal to their market values at the end of their useful lives to your company. The computer system is expected to have little or no market value—obsolescence is the reason. The residual values of the machinery, equipment, furniture, and fixtures are not considered here because they will probably be used beyond the five years covered by this proposal.

10. A capital investment decision is management's act of deciding whether or not to put money into long-term assets for a profit. Capital budgeting is the process of making such a decision. Generally, more than one proposal is considered.

11. Chapter M10 in the textbook contains a discussion of net present value, internal rate of return, payback period, and accounting rate of return.

Sheet 1 data including MACRS tables

	A	B	C	D	E	F	G	H
1								
2			STUDENT'S NAME CORPORATION					
3			CAPITAL INVESTMENT PROPOSAL					
4			TODAY'S DATE					
5		DATA						
6		Cost of machinery & equipment (10-year property)......	$1,100,000					
7		Cost of furniture & fixtures (7-year property).............	$300,000					
8		Cost of computer system (5-year property)..............	$600,000		MACRS Tables For Business Property			
9		Working capital required....................................	$200,000	Recovery	Depreciation Percentages			
10		Annual revenue...	$5,200,000	Year	5-year	7-year	10-year	
11		Cost of goods sold...	60.00%	1	20.00%	14.29%	10.00%	
12		Operating expenses (except depreciation)...............	$1,000,000	2	32.00%	24.49%	18.00%	
13		Federal and state income tax percentage..................	40.00%	3	19.20%	17.49%	14.40%	
14		Required rate of return on investment.....................	15.00%	4	11.52%	12.49%	11.52%	
15		Expected life of investment in years........................	4					
16		Internal rate of return..	15.54612%	Adjust C16 until inflows in C48 equal outflows in C45.				
17								

Sheet 1 calculations

	B	C	D	E	F	G
17						
18	**CALCULATION: NET PRESENT VALUE**	**TODAY**	**YEAR**	**YEAR**	**YEAR**	**YEAR**
19			**1**	**2**	**3**	**4**
20	Cost of machinery & equipment (10-year property)...	($1,100,000)				
21	Cost of furniture & fixtures (7-year property)..............	(300,000)				
22	Cost of computer system (5-year property)..............	(600,000)				
23	Working capital required…...................................	(200,000)				
24	Annual revenue…...		$5,200,000	$5,200,000	$5,200,000	$5,200,000
25	Less cost of goods sold…................................		(3,120,000)	(3,120,000)	(3,120,000)	(3,120,000)
26	Less operating expenses (except depreciation).........		(1,000,000)	(1,000,000)	(1,000,000)	(1,000,000)
27	Less depreciation on 5-year property......................		(120,000)	(192,000)	(115,200)	(69,120)
28	Less depreciation on 7-year property......................		(42,870)	(73,470)	(52,470)	(37,470)
29	Less depreciation on 10-year property...................		(110,000)	(198,000)	(158,400)	(126,720)
30						
31	Annual income before taxes…............................		807,130	616,530	753,930	846,690
32	Less federal and state income taxes......................		(322,852)	(246,612)	(301,572)	(338,676)
33						
34	Annual net income….......................................		484,278	369,918	452,358	508,014
35	Add back depreciation…...................................		272,870	463,470	326,070	233,310
36	Total cash outflow….......................................	(2,200,000)				
37	Annual cash inflows….....................................		757,148	833,388	778,428	741,324
38						
39	Present value of cash inflows…...........................	2,224,234	$658,390	$630,161	$511,829	$423,854
40						
41	Net present value of investment…........................	$24,234				
42						
43	**CALCULATION: INTERNAL RATE OF RETURN**	**TODAY**	**YEAR**	**YEAR**	**YEAR**	**YEAR**
44			**1**	**2**	**3**	**4**
45	Total cash outflow….......................................	($2,200,000)				
46	Annual cash inflows….....................................		$757,148	$833,388	$778,428	$741,324
47						
48	Present value of cash inflows…...........................	$2,200,000	$655,278	$624,218	$504,606	$415,898
49						
50	Internal rate of return…...................................	15.54612%	See note in row 16.			
51						
52	**CALCULATION: PAYBACK PERIOD**	**TODAY**	**YEAR**	**YEAR**	**YEAR**	**YEAR**
53			**1**	**2**	**3**	**4**
54	Total cash outflow….......................................	($2,200,000)				
55	Annual cash inflows….....................................		$757,148	$833,388	$778,428	$741,324
56						
57	Net cash flow…..	($2,200,000)	($1,442,852)	($609,464)	$168,964	$910,288
58						
59	**CALCULATION: ACCOUNTING RATE OF RETURN**	**TODAY**	**YEAR**	**YEAR**	**YEAR**	**YEAR**
60			**1**	**2**	**3**	**4**
61	Total investment…...	$2,200,000				
62	Annual net income….......................................		$484,278	$369,918	$452,358	$508,014
63	Average net income…......................................	$453,642				
64						
65	Accounting rate of return…................................	20.62%				
66						
67	Project 10, Student's Name, Identification Number, Class Number, Today's Date					

Required

Make sure that you complete the following steps in order. Refer to the procedures in the Appendix, which are alphabetized by underlined verb.

1. Open *Excel* and create a worksheet that looks like the example in this project. Use today's actual date in place of the words *today's date* in row 4. Merge and center the text in rows 2 – 4 and row 67. Use cell-based formulas and functions for all calculations. Format the worksheet. Do not use gridlines.
2. Save your worksheet to a floppy disk.
3. Open *Word* and create a report from the notes provided. The report should explain the capital investment proposal on the worksheet. The report title should be *Capital Investment Decisions by Student's Name*. Make sure that your document has an introduction, main body, and conclusion. Keep the introduction short—three sentences will suffice. In the main body, you should discuss the data and the four investment-decision methods. Insert Sheet 1, rows 1 – 17, and discuss the data. Insert Sheet 1, rows 17 – 42, and discuss net present value. Insert Sheet 1, rows 42 – 51, and discuss internal rate of return. Insert Sheet 1, rows 51 – 58, and discuss payback period. Insert Sheet 1, rows 58 – 67, and discuss accounting rate of return. In the conclusion, express an opinion as to which investment-decision method appears to be the best. Indicate why.
4. Insert footers into your *Word* document.
5. Save your *Word* document to a floppy disk.
6. Print your *Word* document and attach it to the back of the Transmittal Sheet.
7. Copy the worksheet.
8. Print the worksheet copy in a format that shows the formulas and functions. Include gridlines and row and column headings. Make sure the worksheet copy fits on one page. Attach the worksheet to the back of the Transmittal Sheet behind the report.
9. Create the table shown below by hand on the Transmittal Sheet. Assume that your marketing department gives the annual revenue goals and the chances of achieving those goals to you. Enter each new revenue amount in cell C10 of the worksheet. Adjust the percentage in cell C16 until the present value of the cash inflows in cell C48 equals the total cash outflow in cell C45. Fill in the remaining boxes on the Transmittal Sheet for each new revenue amount. Write on the Transmittal Sheet whether or not you would invest in this project. Defend your answer.

	$5,200,000	$5,000,000	$4,800,000
Annual revenue goal			
Chance of achieving that goal	90.00%	95.00%	100.00%
Net present value of investment	$24,234		
Internal rate of return	15.54612%		
Payback period (year)	3		
Accounting rate of return	20.62%		

Project Ten Transmittal Sheet

Student Name: _____

Student Identification Number: _____

Class: _____

Date: _____

_____
_____
_____
_____
_____
_____
_____
_____
_____
_____
_____
_____
_____
_____
_____
_____
_____
_____
_____
_____
_____
_____
_____
_____
_____
_____

Notes:

Project Eleven

Internal Control

Competencies

- Integrate *Microsoft® Excel* and *Microsoft® Word* to create a report that discusses internal control areas of concern if a company switches to a management information system that features paperless accounting software.
- Appraise the internal control in a paperless accounting system using a segmented income statement.

Project Data

The worksheet to be used in the report is illustrated below:

	B	C	D	E	F	G	H	I	J	K	L	M	N
1													
2			STUDENT'S NAME CORPORATION										
3			FLASH REPORT										
4			JANUARY 1 THROUGH YESTERDAY, THIS YEAR										
5													
6	DATA	COMPANY	PRODUCT LINES--BUDGETS					COMPANY	PRODUCT LINES--ACTUAL				
7		BUDGET	Custom Widgets		Standard Widgets			ACTUAL	Custom Widgets		Standard Widgets		
8													
9	Sales revenue		$3,300,000		$2,160,000				$3,500,000		$2,120,000		
10	Cost of goods sold		40.0%		30.0%				$1,395,000		$648,000		
11	Other variable exp.		10.0%		10.0%				$421,000		$216,000		
12	Traceable fixed exp.		$900,000		$870,000				$897,000		$868,000		
13	Common fixed exp.	$885,000						$885,000					
14	Income tax exp.	35.0%						$102,000					
15													
16	CALCULATIONS	COMPANY	PRODUCT LINES--BUDGETS					COMPANY	PRODUCT LINES--ACTUAL				
17		BUDGET	Custom Widgets		Standard Widgets			ACTUAL	Custom Widgets		Standard Widgets		
18													
19	Sales revenue	$5,460,000	$3,300,000	100.0%	$2,160,000	100.0%		$5,620,000	$3,500,000	100.0%	$2,120,000	100.0%	
20	Less variable exp.												
21	Cost of goods sold	1,968,000	1,320,000	40.0%	648,000	30.0%		2,043,000	1,395,000	39.9%	648,000	30.6%	
22	Other variable exp.	546,000	330,000	10.0%	216,000	10.0%		637,000	421,000	12.0%	216,000	10.2%	
23													
24	Contribution margin	$2,946,000	$1,650,000	50.0%	$1,296,000	60.0%		$2,940,000	$1,684,000	48.1%	$1,256,000	59.2%	
25	Less traceable fixed exp.	1,770,000	900,000	27.3%	870,000	40.3%		1,765,000	897,000	25.6%	868,000	40.9%	
26													
27	Product line margins	$1,176,000	$750,000	22.7%	$426,000	19.7%		$1,175,000	$787,000	22.5%	$388,000	18.3%	
28	Less common fixed exp.	885,000						885,000					
29													
30	Company margin	$291,000						$290,000					
31	Less income tax exp.	101,850						102,000					
32													
33	Net income	$189,150						$188,000					
34													
35		Project 11, Student's Name, Identification Number, Class Number, Today's Date											

The flash report illustrated is a year-to-date income statement that is segmented by product line. The data section is updated daily from the management information system's paperless accounting software. The calculation section contains an income statement that is segmented by product line. A variable cost of goods sold and a contribution margin are shown rather than an absorption cost of goods sold and a gross margin.

Notes for the report are as follows:

Assume that the management of Student's Name Corporation is looking at a proposed management information system that features paperless accounting software. If the proposed system is adopted, the number of people in the accounting department will drop from fifteen to four—controller, accounts receivable clerk, accounts payable clerk, and payroll clerk. The two internal auditors will also work in the department. They report to the company's audit committee.

The outside auditors (from the CPA firm) suggest that the internal control section of the policies and procedures manual should show the objectives discussed in Chapter M11 of the textbook. The internal controls for the paperless system must be in the manual two years before the corporation goes public (with an initial public offering). The needs for an internal control system remain the same: to protect the company's assets and their efficient use, ensure accurate and reliable information, and encourage adherence to laws and regulations.

Cash procedures changes: The paperless accounting system will have few of the traditional source documents, such as cancelled checks or deposit slips. Most cash receipts from the company's customers will be received by electronic fund transmission directly into the account at the bank. Most cash payments to vendors will be paid by electronic fund transmission. All employees will be paid by electronic fund transmission. All taxes will be paid electronically. The company's bank statements will contain very few cancelled checks or deposit slips.

Accounts receivable procedures changes: The paperless accounting system will have few of the traditional source documents such as customer purchase orders, sales invoices, and sales returns. Most customers will e-mail orders to the company instead of sending purchase orders by surface mail. They will be invoiced by e-mail when the widgets are shipped. A bar code system, offered by the package delivery service, will be used to track goods in transit and deliveries. The primary role of the accounts receivable clerk will be collector of past due balances. The clerk should have a friendly telephone personality. Data entry will be kept to a minimum.

Accounts payable procedures changes: The accounting system will produce few of the traditional source documents such as purchase orders, purchase invoices, proofs of delivery, and purchase returns. Company personnel will e-mail orders to most vendors using an open purchase order number. Delivery dates will coincide with the company's just-in-time manufacturing system. Most vendors will e-mail invoices to the company. Authorization for payment will be done via e-mail. The primary role of the accounts payable clerk will be to train vendors on how to cope with the paperless accounting system. Data entry will be kept to a minimum.

Payroll procedures changes: The accounting system will produce none of the traditional source documents such as tax returns and paychecks. Employees will log in hours using the computer. Supervisors will approve work hours, sick hours, and vacation hours for payment via e-mail. The payroll software will compute gross pay and deductions and compute federal and state payroll tax deposits. The primary roll of the payroll clerk will be to answer employee questions about payroll. Data entry will be kept to a minimum.

Anticipated difficulties with internal control activities: It will be harder to segregate duties such as custody of assets and access to accounting records. There will be fewer people in the accounting department. The recording of most transactions and transfer of most cash will be done by computer. There will be few hard-copy management reports. Flash reports, such as the income statement illustrated, will be available to all employees on the company's internal web site.

Required

> **Make sure that you complete the following steps in order. Refer to the procedures in the Appendix, which are alphabetized by underlined verb. Note the underlined verbs in the steps below.**

1. Open *Excel* and create a worksheet that looks like the example in this project. Use yesterday's actual month, day, and year in the heading. Merge and center the heading and the text in row 35. Use cell-based formulas and functions for all calculations. Format the worksheet to show row and column headings, and gridlines.
2. Open *Word* and create a report with the title *Internal Control, Areas of Concern by Student's Name*. Make sure that your document has an introduction, main body, and conclusion. The report should discuss three or more internal control areas of concern if the corporation switches to a paperless accounting system. Insert *Excel*, cell range A1 – N15, *as a picture* into the *Word* document. Discuss the role of source documents that relate to the data. Insert *Excel*, cell range A15 – N37, *as a picture* into the *Word* document. Discuss the role of hard-copy (printed) reports. The conclusion should contain an opinion about whether or not the company should adopt a paperless accounting system. Chapter M11 in the textbook contains a discussion about internal control.
3. Insert footers into the *Word* document.
4. Save your project to a floppy disk.
5. Print the *Word* document and attach it to the back of the Transmittal Sheet.
6. Copy the worksheet.
7. Print the worksheet copy in a format that shows cell-based formulas.
8. Attach the worksheet copy to the back of the Transmittal Sheet behind the report.
9. Assume that Student's Name Corporation implements the paperless accounting system. Appraise (judge the worth of) the internal control in the hypothetical system using the flash report illustrated in this project. Identify the unexpected actual results for custom widgets and standard widgets when compared to the budgeted amounts.

Project Eleven Transmittal Sheet

Student Name: _____

Student Identification Number: _____

Class: _____

Date: _____

_____
_____
_____
_____
_____
_____
_____
_____
_____
_____
_____
_____
_____
_____
_____
_____
_____
_____
_____
_____
_____
_____

Notes:

Project Twelve

Reciprocal Support Costs

Competencies

- Integrate *Microsoft® Excel* and *Microsoft® PowerPoint* to create a presentation that explains and demonstrates the step-down and simultaneous algebraic equation methods for allocating reciprocal support costs.
- Modify a cost allocation worksheet to include a new revenue-producing department and evaluate the differences in cost allocation using two methods of calculation.

Project Data

Sheet 1:

	A	B	C	D	E	F	G
1							
2		STUDENT'S NAME CORPORATION					
3		COST ALLOCATION WORKSHEET					
4		YEAR ENDED DECEMBER 31, THIS YEAR					
5							
6							
7		COST AND ALLOCATION DATA	SUPPORT DEPARTMENTS		REVENUE DEPARTMENTS		
8			HUMAN	ACCOUNTING	CUSTODIAL	GARDENING	
9			RESOURCES	& PAYROLL	SERVICES	SERVICES	
10		Department costs........................	$400,000	$200,000	$3,200,000	$1,200,000	
11		Human resources allocation.........	-100%	10%	60%	30%	
12		Accounting and payroll allocation...	5%	-100%	45%	50%	
13							
14		STEP-DOWN ALLOCATION	SUPPORT DEPARTMENTS		REVENUE DEPARTMENTS		
15		CALCULATIONS	HUMAN	ACCOUNTING	CUSTODIAL	GARDENING	
16			RESOURCES	& PAYROLL	SERVICES	SERVICES	
17		Beginning balances......................	$400,000	$200,000	$3,200,000	$1,200,000	
18		Human resources allocation..........	(400,000)	40,000	240,000	120,000	
19		Accounting and payroll allocation...	0	(240,000)	113,684	126,316	
20							
21		Ending balances..........................	$0	$0	$3,553,684	$1,446,316	
22							
23		SIMULTANEOUS-EQUATION	SUPPORT DEPARTMENTS		REVENUE DEPARTMENTS		
24		ALLOCATION CALCULATIONS	HUMAN	ACCOUNTING	CUSTODIAL	GARDENING	
25			RESOURCES	& PAYROLL	SERVICES	SERVICES	
26		Beginning balances.......................	$400,000	$200,000	$3,200,000	$1,200,000	
27		Accounting and payroll allocation...	12,060	(241,206)	108,543	120,603	
28		Human resources allocation............	(412,060)	41,206	247,236	123,618	
29							
30		Ending balances..........................	$0	$0	$3,555,779	$1,444,221	
31							
32		**Project 12, Student's Name, Identification Number, Class Number, Today's Date**					

The formula in cell D27 is as follows:

$$=-D10-(C10+C12*D10)/(1-C12*D11)*D11$$

Exhibits of the first slide and last slide are as follows:

Reciprocal Support Costs

By
Student's Name

That's All, Folks!

Required

Make sure that you complete the following steps in order. Refer to the procedures in the Appendix, which are alphabetized by underlined verb. Note the underlined verbs in the steps below.

1. Open *Excel* and create the worksheet illustrated on page 12.1. Merge and center the heading in rows 2 – 4 and the footer in row 32. Use cell-based formulas and functions for all calculations. Format the numbers as shown. Do not format the

worksheet at this time. Use yellow for a fill color. Use blue for a font color. Use a bold font for all text and numbers.

2. Open *PowerPoint* and create a *title slide* using the data in the exhibit.

3. Apply a slide color scheme with a blue background.

4. Insert appropriate slides that will explain and demonstrate the step-down and simultaneous algebraic equation methods illustrated in Chapter M12 of the textbook. Insert Sheet 1, cells A1 – G13, when you discuss the cost and allocation data. Insert Sheet 1, cells A13 – G22, when you discuss the step-down allocation method. Insert Sheet 1, cells A22 – G32, when you discuss the simultaneous-equation allocation method. In your conclusion, indicate which method is better and why. End with the *That's all, folks* slide.

5. Apply *dissolve* as a slide transition effect for slides two through the last slide.

6. Apply *fly from bottom* as text preset animation where appropriate.

7. Apply *speech text* to the slides. Base your speech on information in Chapter M12 of the textbook.

8. Insert footers on the notes pages.

9. Save your project to a floppy disk.

10. Print the presentation as *notes pages* and attach them to the back of the Transmittal Sheet.

11. Copy your worksheet

12. Format Sheet 1 (2)—the worksheet copy. It should show row and column headings, but not the gridlines. Change the fill color to white and the font color to black.

13. Print Sheet 1 (2) showing cell-based formulas and functions. Attach the worksheet to the back of the Transmittal Sheet behind the notes pages.

14. Copy the original worksheet again.

15. Format Sheet 1 (3). It should show row and column headings, but not the gridlines. Change the fill color to white and the font color to black.

16. Modify Sheet 1 (3) to include a new revenue-producing department. Change the cost-allocation calculations as appropriate. The data section of the worksheet is as follows:

A	B	C	D	E	F	G	H
6							
7	COST AND ALLOCATION DATA	SUPPORT DEPARTMENTS		REVENUE DEPARTMENTS			
8		HUMAN	ACCOUNTING	CUSTODIAL	GARDENING	WINDOW	
9		RESOURCES	& PAYROLL	SERVICES	SERVICES	SERVICES	
10	Department costs...........................	$500,000	$300,000	$3,200,000	$2,400,000	$1,200,000	
11	Human resources allocation............	-100%	10%	40%	30%	20%	
12	Accounting and payroll allocation...	5%	-100%	30%	30%	35%	
13							

17. Print your worksheet with the three revenue-producing departments. Attach the worksheet to the back of the Transmittal Sheet behind the notes pages and the worksheet showing cell-based formulas and functions.

18. On the front of the Transmittal Sheet, evaluate the differences in cost allocation using the two methods of calculation. Refer to the sheet that has three revenue-producing departments.

Project Twelve Transmittal Sheet

Student Name: _____

Student Identification Number: _____

Class: _____

Date: _____

_____
_____
_____
_____
_____
_____
_____
_____
_____
_____
_____
_____
_____
_____
_____
_____
_____
_____
_____
_____
_____
_____

Notes:

Group Project Thirteen

Survival Triplet

Competencies

- Integrate *Microsoft® Excel* and *Microsoft® PowerPoint* to create a presentation that describes and charts the elements of the survival triplet and applies what-if analysis of confrontation strategies for three product lines.
- Use *Microsoft® Word* to create a report that describes how three local businesses can use the survival triplet in strategic planning.

Project Data

Sheet 1

	A	B	C	D	E	F	G	H	I
1									
2		GROUP'S NAME CORPORATION							
3		CONFRONTATION STRATEGIES							
4		USING THE SURVIVAL TRIPLET							
5		DECEMBER 31, THIS YEAR							
6									
7		CHART DATA							
8			Max	Min					
9		Price (cost)	0.40	0.20					
10		Functionality	0.30	0.20					
11		Quality	0.30	0.20					
12									
13									
14									
15					Price (cost)				
16					0.40				
17					0.30				
18									
19					0.20			Max	
20					0.10				
21								Min	
22					0.00				
23									
24									
25			Quality			Functionality			
26									
27									
28									
29									
30		Project 13, First Student's Name, Second Student's Name, Third Student's Name, Today's Date							

Chart data changes

For Slide 5:

	A	B	C	D
7		**CHART DATA**		
8			Max	Min
9		Price (cost)	0.40	0.20
10		Functionality	0.30	0.26
11		Quality	0.30	0.26

For Slide 6:

	A	B	C	D
7		**CHART DATA**		
8			Max	Min
9		Price (cost)	0.40	0.36
10		Functionality	0.30	0.16
11		Quality	0.30	0.26

For Slide 7:

	A	B	C	D
7		**CHART DATA**		
8			Max	Min
9		Price (cost)	0.40	0.30
10		Functionality	0.30	0.26
11		Quality	0.30	0.10

Outline of presentation

Slide 1.   Title: Confrontation Strategy
Using the Survival Triplet at
Group's Name Corporation
          Subtitle: By
First Student's Name
Second Student's Name
Third Student's Name

Slide 2.   Title: Topics for Discussion
    Bulleted list: Confrontation strategy at Group's Name Corporation
Three crucial success factors
Our strategy as applied to three product lines

Slide 3.   Title: Confrontation Strategy at
                         Group's Name Corporation
        Bulleted list: A management approach to competition
                         Numerous competitive advantages are created
                         Used when a sustainable competitive advantage is not possible

Slide 4.   Title: Crucial Success Factors

                         [Insert Sheet 1, chart only, into slide 4]

Slide 5.   Title: Our Strategy as Applied to
                         [Insert name of 1st product line]

                         [Insert chart only into slide 5 after data changes are made]

Slide 6.   Title: Our Strategy as Applied to
                         [Insert name of 2nd product line]

                         [Insert chart only into slide 6 after data changes are made]

Slide 7.   Title: Our Strategy as Applied to
                         [Insert name of 3rd product line]

                         [Insert chart only into slide 7 after data changes are made]

Slide 8.   Title: Topics Discussed
        Bulleted list: Confrontation strategy at Group's Name Corporation
                         Three crucial success factors
                         Our strategy as applied to three product lines

Slide 9.   Title: That's All, Folks!

Required

Make sure that you complete the following steps in order. Refer to the procedures in the Appendix, which are alphabetized by underlined verb. Note the underlined verbs in the steps below.

1. Open *Microsoft*® *Excel* according to the procedures in Appendix A. Create a worksheet that looks like the example on page 13.1. Select a group name for your hypothetical company. The name should apply to three related product lines that your company manufactures. Merge and center the text in rows 2 – 5 and 30. Format the worksheet to include row and column headings and gridlines.

2. <u>Save</u> the worksheet to a floppy disk.
3. <u>Open</u> *PowerPoint* and create a *title slide*.
4. <u>Apply</u> a slide color scheme with a blue background and yellow and white font colors.
5. <u>Insert</u> a *bulleted list* format for slides 2, 3, and 8.
6. <u>Insert</u> a *title only* format for slides 4 – 7 and 9. Select three related product lines that could correspond to the chart data changes in slides 5 – 7. Use familiar product lines that group members purchase often.
7. <u>Insert</u> an *Excel* chart into *PowerPoint* slide 4. Remember to change the chart data before inserting the chart into each of slides 5 – 7.
8. <u>Apply</u> *dissolve* as a slide transition effect for slides 2 – 9.
9. <u>Apply</u> *fly from bottom* as text preset animation for slides 2, 3, and 8.
10. <u>Apply</u> a *speech text* to slides 1 – 9. Use Chapter M13 in the textbook as a source of information.
11. <u>Insert</u> footers on the notes pages. The footers should include Project 13, names of students in the group, and today's date.
12. <u>Save</u> your presentation to a floppy disk.
13. <u>Print</u> the slides as notes pages.
14. <u>Print</u> the worksheet and attach it to the back of the notes pages.
15. <u>Open</u> *Microsoft*® *Word* and create a report that describes how three local businesses can use the survival triplet in strategic planning. Select businesses where you work or are regular customers. The report title should be:

How Businesses Can Use The Survival Triplet

By

First Student's Name

Second Student's Name

Third Student's Name

16. Make sure that your document has an introduction, main body, and conclusion. It should be double-spaced. <u>Insert</u> a footer into your *Word* document. The footer should include the following:

Project 13, Student Names, Class Number, Today's Date

17. <u>Save</u> your document to a data disk.
18. Attach the report to the back of the notes pages.

Appendix

Procedures for *Excel, PowerPoint & Word*

> **The procedures for completing projects in this workbook are alphabetized by underlined verb. The procedures are for *Microsoft® Office 2000* software. Most procedures work with *Microsoft® Office '97* software.**

<u>Apply</u> a *slide color scheme* in a *PowerPoint* presentation

    Click on the **Format** menu
    Click on the **Slide Color Scheme** menu selection
    Click on the **Color Scheme** with the blue background
    Click on the **Apply To All** button

<u>Apply</u> borders in *Excel*

Create the following worksheet:

	A	B	C
1			
2			
3		How to Put Borders	
4		In a Worksheet	
5			
6			

Apply borders as follows:

    Drag cell **B2** through cell **B5**

    Note: Instructions for dragging cell B2 through cell B5 are as follows: Move your mouse until the Cross icon is in cell B2. (The Cross icon is the moving graphic image on your computer screen that looks like a cross.) Hold the left-hand button of the mouse down while you move the mouse until the Cross icon is in cell B5. Release the mouse button.

    Click on the **Format** menu and on the **Cells** menu command
    Click on the **Border** tab and click on the **Thickest Line** in the **Style** box
    Click on the **Top**, **Bottom**, **Left**, and **Right** border buttons
    Click on the **OK** button

Apply colors in *Excel*

Create the following worksheet:

	A	B	C
1			
2			
3		How to Put Colors	
4		In a Worksheet	
5			
6			

Apply colors as follows:

Drag cell **B2** through cell **B5**
Click on the **Font** tab
Click on the **Down Arrow** on the right side of the **Color** box
Click on the **Blue** color patch
Click on the **Patterns** tab and click on the **Yellow** color patch
Click on the **OK** button and click on cell **A1** to see the results

Apply *dissolve* as a slide transition effect in *PowerPoint*

Click on the **View** menu
Click on the **Slide Sorter** menu selection and click on **Slide 2** to highlight
Click on the **Down Arrow** button in the **Slide Transition Effects** box
Click on the right-hand **Down Arrow** button in **Slide Transition Effects** box
Click on the **Dissolve** menu command

Apply *fly from bottom* as text preset animation in *PowerPoint*

Click on the **View** menu (unless you have already done this)
Click on the **Slide Sorter** menu selection (unless you have already done this)
Click on **Slide 2** to highlight
Click on the **Down Arrow** button in the **Text Preset Animation** box
Click on the **Fly From Bottom** menu command

Apply *speech text* to slides in a *PowerPoint* presentation

> Click on the **View** menu
> Click on the **Notes Page** menu selection
> Press the **PageUp** key as often as you need to get to Slide 1
> Click in the **Click to Add Text** box
> Click on the **Down Arrow** key on the right side of the **Font Size** box
> Click on size **20** and type the portion of the speech that applies to this slide
> Press the **PageDown** key to advance to the next slide

Copy an *Excel* worksheet

Do the following to make a copy of the *Sheet 2* worksheet:

> Click on the **Edit** menu
> Click on the **Move or Copy Sheet** menu command
> Click inside the **Create A Copy** box and on the **OK** button

The tab name for the copy of the *Sheet 2* worksheet is *Sheet 2 (2)*.

Create a *chart* in an *Excel* worksheet

Enter and format the following chart calculations:

	A	B	C	D	E	F	G	H	I	J	K
1											
2		**COMMON STOCK MARKET PRICES**									
3											
4		Corporation name: SAMPLE CORPORATION									
5			1Q1999	2Q1999	3Q1999	4Q1999	1Q2000	2Q2000	3Q2000	4Q2000	
6		Mkt High	$27.75	$24.06	$20.50	$19.00	$31.91	$27.67	$23.58	$21.85	
7		Mkt Low	$22.38	$17.38	$16.88	$13.00	$25.73	$19.98	$19.41	$14.95	
8											

Highlight the chart calculations as follows:

> Drag cell **B5** to cell **J7**

Create a chart as follows:

> Click on the **Insert** file
> Click on the **Chart** menu selection
> Click on **Bar** in the **Chart Type** box
> Click on the **Next** button *three* times
> Click on the **Finish** button

Reposition the chart as follows:

> Move the **Arrow** icon inside the chart area
> Keep the **Left** mouse button down
> Move the mouse until the **Upper-Left** corner of the chart is in cell **B9**
> Release the **Left** mouse button
> Move the **Arrow** icon over the **Bottom** square along the **Right** line of the chart
>
> **Note: The Arrow icon will change to a Double-Arrow icon when it is properly placed.**
>
> Keep the **Left** mouse button down
> Move the mouse until the **Right** line of the chart is on the **Right** side of worksheet column J and release the mouse button

Enter a *cell-based formula* in an *Excel* worksheet

Cells that show calculations are *formula driven*. Formula driven means that the calculations contain cell locations where the data is stored rather than the actual data. To demonstrate a cell-based formula, open a new workbook and do the following:

> Click on the **Sheet 1** tab and click on cell **B4**
> Type **125** in cell **B4** and press the **Enter** key
> Type **20** in cell **B5** and press the **Enter** key

Assume that you want to show the product of the amounts in cell B4 and B5 of Sheet 1 in cell C6 of Sheet 2. The product of 125 times 20 is 2,500. Enter your formula as follows:

> Click on the **Sheet 2** tab and click on cell **C6**
> In cell **C6**, press the = (equal) key and click on the **Sheet 1** tab
> Click on cell **B4** and press the * (multiply) key
> Click on cell **B5** and press the **Enter** key

Enter a *SUM function* in an *Excel* worksheet

A SUM function is a prewritten formula that takes positive and negative values, performs an operation, and returns a value (displays a total). Enter numbers in cells B2 through B4 according to the following illustration:

	A	B	C
1			
2		3000	
3		-1500	
4		4000	
5			

The function that you enter in cell B6 should equal 5500. Do the following:

> Drag cell **B2** through cell **B6**
> Click on the **AutoSum** button (with the Greek letter *Sigma* on it) on the tool bar

<u>Enter</u> and format a *dollar amount* in an *Excel* worksheet

> In cell **C11**, type **1875** using the ten-key pad and press the **Enter** key
> Click on cell **C11** to make it the active cell
> Click on the **Format** menu
> Click on the **Cells** menu selection
> Click on **Currency** in the **Category** box
> Double click on the **Down Arrow** button on right side of the **Decimal Places** box
> Click on **Down Arrow** button on right side of **Symbol** box
> Click on the **$** sign
> Click on **($1,234)** in the **Negative Numbers** box
> Click on the **OK** button

<u>Enter</u> and format a *number* in an *Excel* worksheet

> In cell **C12**, type **1875** using the ten-key pad and press the **Enter** key
> Click on cell **C12** to make it the active cell
> Click on the **Format** menu
> Click on the **Cells** menu selection
> Click on **Number** in the **Category** box
> Double click the **Down Arrow** button on right side of the **Decimal Places** box
> Click inside the **Use 1000 Separator** box
> Click on **(1,234)** in the **Negative Numbers** box
> Click on the **OK** button

<u>Enter</u> the date as text in an *Excel* worksheet

> Click on cell **A4**
>
> Note: Make sure that you type an apostrophe before the word *December* in the procedure below. The apostrophe causes the software to treat the date as ordinary text. Use the actual year in place of the words *this year*.
>
> In cell **A7**, type 'DECEMBER 31, THIS YEAR and press the **Enter** key

<u>Exit</u> your project

Make sure that you save your project to your data disk before you exit. Exit the project as follows:

> Click on the **File** menu, then on the **Exit** menu selection

Click on the **Yes** button if you are asked if you want to save changes
Remove your floppy disk if you are through for the day

Your instructor should have specific instructions for shutting down your computer.

Format a floppy disk

Format a blank floppy disk according to the procedures in the handout provided by your instructor. If no handout is provided, do the following:

Insert a disk into the drive
Double click on the **My Computer** icon
Click on the **3½ Floppy** option and click on the **File** menu
Click on the **Format** menu selection and click on the **Start** button
Click on the two **Close** buttons when the formatting is complete

Format an *Excel* worksheet column width

Assume that you are formatting the column B width to 30. Do the following:

Click on any cell in column **B** and click on the **Format** menu name
Arrow to the **Column** menu selection and click on the **Width** menu command
Type 30 in the **Column width** box and click on the **OK** button

Format each *Excel* worksheet

Click on the **File** menu, then on the **Page Setup** menu selection
Click on the **Page** tab and on the **Fit To** button
Click on the **Margins** tab
Click in the **Horizontally** box to add a checkmark
Click on the **Sheet** tab
Click in the **Gridlines** box to add a checkmark
Click in the **Row And Column Headings** box to add a checkmark
Click on the **OK** button

Format numbers in an *Excel* worksheet

See <u>enter</u> and format numbers.

Insert a *bulleted-list* or *title only* format in *PowerPoint*

Assume that you opened *PowerPoint* and created the *Title Slide* for a presentation. Do the following to insert a *Bulleted-List* or *Title-Only* slide:

Click on the **Insert** menu and the **New Slide** menu option

Click on the **Bulleted List** option that is shown in the **Auto Layout** box,
   or click on the **Title Only** option (3rd row down, 3rd option from left)
Click the **OK** button

Insert a fourth worksheet into an *Excel* workbook

Click on the **Insert** menu
Click on the **Worksheet** menu command
Click on the **Edit** menu name
Click on the **Move or Copy Sheet** menu command
Click on **(move to end)** and the **OK** button

Insert an *Excel* chart into a *PowerPoint* slide

Create the following worksheet with chart:

	A	B	C	D	E	F	G	H	I
1	Chart Data								
2		Max	Min						
3	Price (cost)	0.40	0.20						
4	Functionality	0.30	0.20						
5	Quality	0.30	0.20						

Click inside the chart area and click on the **Copy** button
Click on the **PowerPoint** tab and click in the gray area outside the slide
Click on the **Paste** button

Position the chart inside the slide as follows:

Move the mouse icon inside the chart
Keep the left mouse button down and move the mouse to move the
    chart to the upper-left corner of the slide under the title
Release the left mouse button

Position the mouse icon over the lower-right corner of the chart
Keep the left mouse button down and move the mouse to stretch the
    chart to the lower-right corner of the slide
Release the right mouse button

Insert an *Excel* worksheet cell range into a *PowerPoint* slide

Create the following worksheet:

	A	B	C	D
1				
2		Sales revenue.........................	$1,200,000	
3		Cost of goods sold..................	$800,000	
4				
5		Gross margin...........................	$400,000	
6		Operating expenses..................	$350,000	
7				
8		Net income.............................	$50,000	
9				

Drag cell **A1** through cell **D9** and click on the **Copy** button
Click on the **PowerPoint** tab and click in the gray area outside the slide
Click on the **Paste** button

Position the worksheet inside the slide as follows:

Move the mouse icon inside the worksheet
Keep the left mouse button down and move the mouse to move the
    worksheet to the upper-left corner of the slide under the title
Release the left mouse button

Position the mouse icon over the lower-right corner of the worksheet
Keep the left mouse button down and move the mouse to stretch the
    worksheet to the lower-right corner of the slide
Release the right mouse button

Insert an *Excel* worksheet cell range into a *Word* document

Create the following worksheet:

	A	B	C	D
1				
2		Sales revenue........................	$1,200,000	
3		Cost of goods sold..................	$800,000	
4				
5		Gross margin..........................	$400,000	
6		Operating expenses.................	$350,000	
7				
8		Net income.............................	$50,000	
9				

Type the following in a *Word* document:

> The sales revenue is the largest amount on an income statement.
>
> [Insert Sheet 1, cells A1 – D9, *as a picture*]
>
> The net income is the bottom line of an income statement.

Copy the worksheet cell range as follows:

> Click on the *Excel* worksheet tab
> Drag cell **A1** through cell **D9** of the worksheet and click on the **Copy** button
> Click on the *Word* document tab
> Highlight **[Insert Sheet 1, cells A1 – D9]** and press the **Delete** key
> Click on the **Edit** menu and the **Paste Special** menu selection
> Click on **Picture** in the **As** box and click on the **OK** button

Insert *footers* into the *Word* document

> Click on the **View** menu
> Click on the **Header and Footer** menu selection
> Click on the **Switch Between Header and Footer** button

> Note: In the following instruction, use the actual project number in place of #. Use your first and last names in place of the words *student's name*. Use your student identification number in place of the words *identification number*. Use your actual class number or class day and time in place of the words *class number*. Use today's actual date rather than the words *today's date.*

Type **Project #, student's name, identification number, class number,**
     today's date and press the **Enter** key
Click on the **Close** button

Insert *footers* into the *PowerPoint* notes pages

Click on the **View** menu
Click on the **Header and Footer** menu selection
Click on the **Notes and Handouts** tab
Click in the box below **Footer**

Note: In the instruction below, use the actual project number in place of the #. Use your first and last names in place of the words *student's name*. Use your student identification number in place of the words *identification number*. Use your actual class number or class day and time in place of the words *class number*. Use today's actual date rather than the words *today's date*.

Type **Project #, student's name, identification number, class number,**
     today's date and press the **Enter** key
Click on the **Apply to All** button

Merge and center text in an *Excel* Worksheet

Note: Use your actual name in place of the words *student's name* below.

Type **STUDENT'S NAME CORPORATION** in cell **A2**
     and press the **Enter** key
Drag cell **A2** to cell **I2** and click on the **Merge and Center** button

Open an existing file

Open a project file according to the procedures in the handout provided by your instructor. If no handout is provided, do the following:

Double click on the **My Computer** icon
Double click on the **3½ Floppy** option
Double click on **01JA4444** (or your project file name)

Another way to open your file is as follows:

Click on the **Start** button and move the **Arrow** icon to the **Programs** option
Click on the appropriate program and click on the **Open** button
Click on the **More Files** option if necessary and click the **OK** button
Click on the **Down Arrow** button on the right side of the **Look In** box
Click on **3½ Floppy (A:)** and click on your project file name

Open *Excel*

> Click on the **Start** button (in the lower left corner of your screen)
> Click on **Programs** and click on **Microsoft Excel**

Sheet 1, the active worksheet of the new workbook that you just opened, appears on your computer screen. This worksheet consists of vertical columns that are lettered and horizontal rows that are numbered. The intersection of a particular column and row is called a *cell*. The active cell of a newly opened worksheet is always cell A1. It is the intersection of column A and row 1. Sheet 1 is located inside a large box called a *window*.

Open *PowerPoint* and create a *title slide*

Open a new presentation as follows:

> Click on the **Start** button (in the lower left corner of your screen)
> Click on **Programs** and click on **Microsoft PowerPoint**
> Click on **Blank Presentation** and click on the **OK** button

At this point the title slide option is highlighted in the Auto-Layout box

> Click on the **OK** button
> Click in the **click to add title** box and enter the title of your presentation
> Click in the **click to add subtitle** box
> Type **By** and press the **Enter** key
>
> **Note: Use your first and last name in place of the words Student's Name in the instruction below.**
>
> Enter **Student's Name**

Open *Word* and format a new document

Do the following:

> Click on the **Start** button
> Click on **Programs** and click on **Microsoft Word**
> Click on the **File** menu
> Click on the **Page Setup** menu selection
> Click on the **Margins** tab
> Verify that the margins are **1"** all around
> Verify that the footer is **0.5"** from the bottom edge
> Click on the **OK** button

Format the document for double-spaced lines (if requested):

Click on the **Format** menu name and click on the **Paragraph** menu selection
Click on the **Down Arrow** button on the right side of the **Line Spacing** box
Click on **Double** and click on the **OK** button

Preview an *Excel* worksheet

You can do your part for ecology by always previewing a worksheet before you print it. If you correct your errors before wasting paper, you'll eventually save a tree. Do the following to preview your worksheet:

Click on the **Print Preview** button (it looks like a page with a magnifying glass)
Click on the **Zoom** button
Press the **Arrow** keys to move around your worksheet
Click on the **Close** button when you are through inspecting your worksheet

Print each *Excel* worksheet copy to show the formulas

Click on the **Tools** menu
Click on the **Options** menu selection
Click in the **Formulas** box under **Windows Options**
Click on the **OK** button
Adjust column widths (See **Format** an Excel worksheet column width if necessary)
Click on **Print** button to print each worksheet copy

Print an *Excel* workbook

Print all worksheets in your workbook as follows:

Click on the **File** menu
Click on the **Print** menu selection
Click on **Entire workbook** and press the **Enter** key

Print a *PowerPoint* presentation as *notes pages*

Click on the **File** menu
Click on the **Print** menu selection
Click on the **Down Arrow** button on the right side of the **Print What** box
Click on the **Notes Pages** command and click on the **OK** button

Print a *Word* document

Click on the **File** menu
Click on the **Print** menu selection
Click on the **OK** button

Save your project to a floppy disk

Your instructor may have specific instructions for saving your project as a file on a floppy disk. If he or she does not, do the following:

Insert your *formatted* floppy disk in the **A** drive of your computer
Click on the **File** menu name and click on the **Save As** menu command
Click on the **Down Arrow** button on the right side of the **Save In** box
Click on the **3½ Floppy (A:)** option
Click inside the **File Name** box to the right of the **Book1** file name
Press the **Backspace** key five times to remove the file name

Note: Assume this is Project One so use the numbers *01* below. Use the initials of your name in place of the initials *SN*. Also, use the last four digits of your student identification number in place of the numbers *4444*. If, for example, your name is *Student Name* and your student identification number is *333-22-4444*, you would enter *01SN4444* as a file name.

Type **01SN4444** and click on the **Save** button